40th State to join the Union

SCENE: MOUNT RUSHMORE.
STATE FLOWER: PASQUE.
STATE FLAG.
FAMOUS PERSON: CHIEF SITTING BULL.

SOUTH DAKOTA
by Nancy Veglahn

Nancy Veglahn sees South Dakota as a "state of infinite variety." Its rich farms in the east and its wide-open grazing lands in the center of the state are seen in sharp contrast with its mysterious Badlands in the majestic Black Hills in the west. Cowboys still herd cattle on horseback; Deadwood and Boot Hill are reminders of the gold rush days, and vast Indian reservations preserve the traditions of the Dakota Sioux.

Yet South Dakota is rapidly moving into the twentieth century. Farmers and ranchers use complex machinery and methods to raise the cattle, corn, and grain that are basic to the state's economy. Four large dams on the Missouri River now produce large amounts of hydroelectric power, and the resulting "Great Lakes of South Dakota" promise to provide major areas for recreation and commercial fishing.

Mrs. Veglahn's account (prepared in consultation with Olive S. Berg, director of curriculum of the South Dakota State Department of Public Instruction) admirably surveys the history, resources, and present-day economy of South Dakota in an absorbing manner that will delight all young readers.

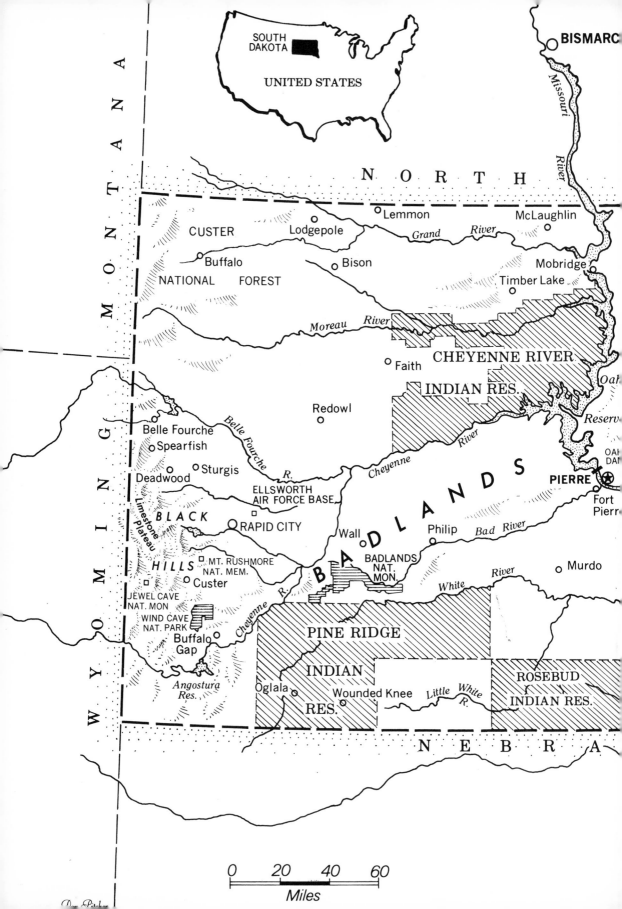

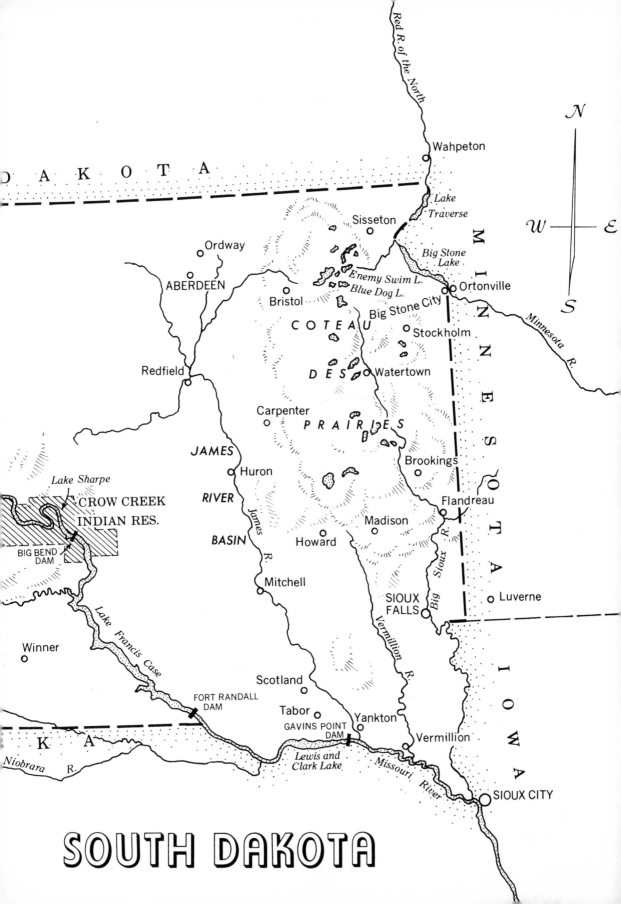

SOUTH DAKOTA

SOUTH

CONSULTANT: **Olive S. Berg**
Formerly Director of Curriculum
State Department of Public Instruction
Pierre, South Dakota

STATES OF THE NATION

DAKOTA

by Nancy Veglahn

COWARD-McCANN, INC.   NEW YORK

PHOTO CREDITS

Black Hills Passion Play of America, page 62
Chamber of Commerce, Deadwood, South Dakota, page 60
Chamber of Commerce, Mitchell, South Dakota, page 25
Department of Interior, Bureau of Indian Affairs, pages 88, 89, 93, 96, 98
Homestake Mining Co., Lead, South Dakota, pages 67, 68, 69, 72
National Park Service, pages 54, 74, 75
Sky Ranch Foundation, pages 45, 110
Smithsonian Institution, page 85
South Dakota Department of Game, Fish and Parks, pages 11, 17, 32, 33, 42, 77
South Dakota Department of Highways, pages 19, 51, 52, 57, 79, 80, 82, 83, 104, 105, 113
South Dakota State University, pages 22, 28, 36, 37, 39, 46, 47, 101, 106
U.S. Army Engineer District, Omaha Corps of Engineers, title page; pages 9, 12, 13, 14, 109
U.S. Forest Service
Wall Drug, Ted Husted, page 20

Jacket

Mount Rushmore: South Dakota Department of Highways
Pasque: South Dakota Department of Highways
State Flag: F. E. Compton & Company
Chief Sitting Bull: New York Public Library

Maps, Donald T. Pitcher
Title page, Fort Randall Dam
Page 19, from "The Free Wind," from *Sun and Saddle Leather.* Copyright 1962 by Dakota Wesleyan University. Reprinted by permission of Dakota Wesleyan University.
Page 30, Copyright 1967 by *South Dakota Conservation Digest.* Reprinted by permission of the South Dakota Department of Game Fish and Parks.

Contents

Chapter 1

The River

Today, the Big Muddy is gone.

For centuries the Missouri River wound through the prairies of the northern plains, dominating the landscape.

Indians built villages along its banks. When Lewis and Clark began their exploration of the Louisiana Purchase they used the Missouri as their pathway. Fur trappers and traders sang as they paddled down the course of the river:

> O Shenandoah, I long to see you.
> Away! you rolling river.
> O Shenandoah, I long to see you.
> Away, we're bound away.
> Across the wide Missouri.

8

Oahe Dam.

It was known as the Big Muddy because so much silt was suspended in the water that light could penetrate only a few inches. Most species of fish were unable to adapt to the murky water environment. Frequent floods destroyed crops of the homesteaders who settled along the river.

South Dakota is still divided into two parts by the waterway known as the Missouri River. But the Big Muddy is gone. A system of huge earth dams has transformed the old, wild river into a series of blue lakes teeming with fish and controlled by men.

South Dakota is a state of contrasts and contradictions. A river that is no longer a river, cowboys in station wagons, ancient Sioux chants and modern jazz, wood-burning stoves and atomic power: these are pieces of the puzzle.

The changes which have taken place on the Missouri have created some of the biggest surprises. Most people think of South Dakota as a landlocked state, almost a desert. Yet South Dakotans own the most boats per capita in the nation! Once miners and homesteaders used the Missouri for transportation. Today it provides electric power, water for irrigation, fishing for food and sport, and a coastline almost as long as the combined coasts of Washington, Oregon, and California.

The four dams which tamed the Missouri in South Dakota are Fort Randall Dam near Pickstown (1952), Gavins Point Dam at Yankton (1955), Oahe Dam at Pierre (1958), and Big Bend Dam at Fort Thompson (1963).

Oahe, built near the state capital, is the world's second largest earthen dam. The lake backed up by the dam extends 250 miles to near Bismarck, North Dakota.

South of Pierre along the old course of the Missouri, the Big Bend Dam created Lake Sharpe in the center of the Crow Creek and Lower Brule Indian reservations. Only a short distance south of Big Bend is Lake Frances Case, the reservoir of Fort Randall Dam. The long waterway continues through Lewis and Clark Lake and finally ends at Gavins Point Dam near Yankton in the southeast corner of the state.

Together these four dams and their reservoirs make up the "Great

Sylvan Lake, Black Hills, South Dakota

Lakes of South Dakota." Because the water moves much more slow-
ly than before, most of the silt that gave the Big Muddy its nick-
name has settled to the bottom. A thousand square miles of blue
water now lie between the northern and southern borders of the
state.

It will take time for South Dakota to develop all the possibilities
of its Great Lakes. Lewis and Clark Lake, in the more heavily populated southeast corner of the state, is already a popular recreation
area. Fishermen near Pierre catch more than thirty different species,

11

from the relatively common northern pike to the prehistoric paddle-fish, which is found only in the Missouri and Yangtze River in China. One of these paddlefish caught near Oahe Dam weighed 90 pounds.

Millions of ducks fill the South Dakota skies in the spring and fall. Many of them stop over along the Missouri reservoirs, making these excellent spots for duck hunters. Other South Dakotans who do not care to hunt the beautiful mallards simply watch them flying high overhead or swimming by the thousands in the new lakes.

The Missouri was harnessed through the Pick-Sloan Plan, developed by the U.S. Army Corps of Engineers and the Department of the Interior. Six dams have been built along the course of the Missouri since World War II, four of them in South Dakota.

The four South Dakota dams can store some 10,000,000,000,000 gallons of water. This would be enough to fill a canal 1,000 feet wide and 100 feet deep from New York to San Francisco.

There is something strange and raw about the new lakes. The riverbanks carved through hundreds of years have been covered over. Now the wide, wild ranchland drops abruptly into the expanse of water. Newly built bridges span the river with scarcely a house or store in sight.

Near Mobridge in north-central South Dakota the frontier town of LeBeau, like river towns, was flooded by the backwaters of Oahe Dam. Once a large, bustling cattle market, LeBeau is gone forever. In its heyday in the early 1900's LeBeau shipped as many as 150,000 head of cattle out of South Dakota each year.

Only a short distance north of LeBeau was an ancient Ree Indian village. Archeologists found many Indian artifacts—spears, pottery, arrowheads and tools—on the site of this 500-year-old village. Now it, too, has been doomed by the Oahe Dam.

So the two will lie side by side beneath the water, Indian village and cow town, with no sign that either of them ever existed. Now there is only the silence of deep water, endless sky and rolling prairie.

Old places and old customs must give way to the future, in South Dakota as everywhere. The Big Muddy is gone, and with it much that was once a way of life. The changes brought about by the taming of the Missouri are only beginning. Yet it still lies along its former course, belonging both to the past and the future.

Like the river, South Dakota is changing. People are moving from farms to cities. New industries are being developed. Missile installations dot the grassland of the west. But everywhere are reminders of what used to be.

Ducks in flight, Gavins Point Dam

Pike caught in Fort Randall tailwaters

Even the names of South Dakota communities can tell something of the past. Fort Pierre, Flandreau and Belle Fourche recall the French traders who were the first white men to explore the area. Many of the settlers of eastern South Dakota were of English or Scottish origin, and they named their towns Aberdeen, Scotland, Carpenter, Bristol.

Stockholm was founded by Swedes, Bergen by Norwegians. Buffalo, Bison and Buffalo Gap are reminders of the huge animals that onced roamed these plains. Murdo, Lemmon and Philip were named for early-day ranchers who developed herds of beef cattle.

Many South Dakota names come from those who first possessed the land—the Indians. "Dakota" is part of the tribal name of the Teton Dakota branch of the Sioux Indians. The towns of Sisseton, Yankton, Huron and Oglala are named for individual Dakota tribes.

Sioux Falls, Lodgepole, Wounded Knee, Red Owl—all point to the fact that this was once Indian territory, and not so long ago.

In South Dakota, real cowboys and real Indians are still very much a part of the scene. Herds of cattle graze across hundreds of miles of prairie, much as they did in the days of the longhorns and stage-coaches. The state is less than a hundred years old, and there are people alive who remember its beginnings.

But the currents of the twentieth century have not left South Dakota untouched. The Missouri will never be the same. Farmers use complicated machinery and study economic trends. Ranchers from remote areas fly to Minneapolis or Chicago for the weekend. Jets from Ellsworth Air Force Base near Rapid City fly over cattle ranches and Indian reservations.

There are many interesting things to see and do in South Dakota, but somehow all journeys must start with the river.

South Dakotans think of their state as divided into two distinct parts: East-river and West-river. And these parts are, indeed, very different.

Looking east from the Missouri at Pierre, you can see the begin-ning of the farmland of South Dakota. The eastern part of the state really belongs to the middle western United States. Like Iowa and Minnesota, it is a land of gently rolling plains, with neat farms and small towns at most of the crossroads.

West-river is part of the American West. Look west from Pierre and you see stretches of empty, rugged land. This is ranch country, cattle country. It is common to drive for 50 miles without going through a town. Much of the land is part of four large Indian re-servations. The rest is used for cattle, sheep, and even a few small herds of buffalo. At the extreme western edge of the state rise the Black Hills, with their granite peaks and acres of forest.

It is the river that divides South Dakota, and at the same time the Missouri, winding through the state like a crooked spine, holds it together.

The Big Muddy is gone, but the Missouri is still there. Like South Dakota, it is both old and new, changing and unchangeable, full of promise.

15

Chapter 2

The Clean, Free Wind

How about going to town for a cup of coffee?" a rancher asks his wife.

"Sure, good idea, I'll be ready in a minute."

They climb into the family pickup truck and drive into Wall to have coffee at the famous drugstore there. The trip is not especially long by South Dakota standards— 45 miles from the ranch to town.

Driving almost a hundred miles for a cup of coffee is not unusual in a state of long distances, sparse population and little traffic. South Dakotans use the stretches of open road to shop, do business or visit with little thought for the number of miles driven in a day.

Wall Drug is a minor American legend that laughs at distance.

Friends of Ted Husted, the owner, have posted thousands of signs all over the world advertising his small-town drugstore on the western plains of South Dakota.

16

Pine-covered buttes in northwestern South Dakota

Cliff Foss of Sioux Falls put a sign on the door of a snow-covered igloo in Point Barrow, Alaska, which reads: *4,500 miles to Wall Drug Store, Wall, South Dakota*. A former Wall resident, Bud Deutscher, put a sign at an International Geophysical Year scientific research station near the North Pole: *3,400 miles to Wall Drug*. Other signs have been posted in Shanghai, China; on the 38th parallel in Korea; and even near India's Taj Mahal.

Pictures on the wall of the restaurant area of the drugstore show signs which have been posted all over the United States and the world by friends and customers. Every year thousands of customers take Wall Drug signs home with them to Maine, Virginia, Oregon, California; and most of them mail back a picture of the sign when it has been erected.

Wall Drug is not just a small-town drugstore anymore. It takes a crew of 120 employees to run the store in the summer when it swarms with tourists on their way to the Black Hills. Among its wares are western clothes, souvenirs, rocks, books and postcards, and meals.

But in the winter the store belongs to South Dakotans again, and they come for miles to have coffee, exchange news and talk things over. This is one of the ways in which South Dakota people overcome the isolation and loneliness of their big, open country.

Although it ranks sixteenth among the states in land area, South Dakota is fortieth in population. With only about nine people per square mile, it is the least densely populated state east of the Rocky Mountains.

A carload of tourists from New York or Pennsylvania may be terrified by the seeming emptiness of the land. One such group of visiters recently stopped at a ranch in the northwest corner of the state and asked with a sort of panic, "How long does this go *on*?"

Yet to those who live in South Dakota the emptiness is not frightening. They like to be able to see for miles in any direction; they like the clean air and the quiet and the elbowroom they have. Watching a herd of deer cross the road at sunset or a pheasant strutting in a cornfield, they do not envy the crowded cities.

Badger Clark was a man who grew up in the Black Hills of South Dakota, worked as a cowpuncher and later wrote some of his feelings

Badger Clark

and experiences in poetry. He loved the hills and prairies of his native state and had a knack for catching the essence of their beauty, as in his poem "The Free Wind":

> And the wind, the wind, the clean free wind,
> She laughed through the April rains:
> Come out and live by the wine I give
> In the smell of the greenin' plains!

The wind has not always been welcome in South Dakota. In the "dirty thirties" it carried clouds of dust and ravenous grasshoppers. And sometimes in winter it brings paralyzing drifts of snow. It can make a lonely sound, whining around the corners of a house isolated by darkness and miles from the nearest neighbor. But the wind is a part of life in the Great Plains, and it can be gentle.

At one time South Dakota was part of the so-called Great American Desert. Until after the Civil War the western United States was designated in that way in school geographies. The area was considered too dry and barren for cultivation.

Wall Drug Store, Wall, South Dakota

A hundred years ago an Ohio Congressman, James Ashley, proposed in the U.S. House of Representatives that Dakota Territory be given back to the Indians. "Dakota is worthless for agriculture," he declared, "and must for a century, at least, remain Indian territory."

Actually, the soil of South Dakota is as rich as any in the world. The problem is water. The average rainfall in the state is about 20 inches per year, although this varies a great deal. In the southeastern part of the state rainfall is usually heaviest, and there farmers raise excellent crops of corn and wheat on the clay loam soil. Moving

20

west, rainfall becomes lighter and more uncertain. Soil in the central part of South Dakota around Pierre is a sticky gumbo which is hard to cultivate but good for cattle grazing.

Although the general division of East-river and West-river is commonly used, there are really three South Dakotas.

The first major part of the state is known as the Prairie Plains, roughly the area east of the Missouri. Within the Prairie Plains are the heavily populated areas around Sioux Falls and Yankton; the James River basin which extends the length of the state; and the Coteau des Prairies area of natural lakes in the northeast.

The Prairie Plains are an extension of the great midwestern farm belt. The land is flat or gently rolling, the soil rich, the major occupation farming, and the towns typical of rural areas in any of the midwestern states.

From the Missouri west runs the second part of South Dakota: the Great Plains. Here there are wide, level stretches of land but also hills, gorges and buttes. The countryside is mostly grassland. The Grand, Moreau, Cheyenne and White rivers cut deep gullies through the land. Deer, pronghorn antelope, prairie dogs and jack-rabbits live among the herds of cattle. The fantastic Badlands contain prehistoric fossils and unearthly rock formations.

In extreme western South Dakota is the third section of the state, the Black Hills. These "hills" are really an extension of the Rocky Mountains. They contain thousands of acres of pine forest, spectacular peaks, and, below the surface, the richest gold mine in the western hemisphere.

Prairie Plains, Great Plains and Black Hills: three different South Dakotas. They are bound together by a common state government, the river, and the clean, free wind.

South Dakota is usually considered semiarid. One of the popular nicknames of South Dakota is the Sunshine State. There are four distinct seasons in the year, each with its own beauty and its own problems.

Winters may be hard, not so much because of heavy snow or low temperatures as because of the isolation of homes in some parts of the state. A South Dakotan rarely starts a winter trip without

South Dakota snowfall

blankets, food and medical supplies in the back of his car. Blizzards can come up without warning, and a car may be stranded 10 miles from the nearest home or store.

In summer people watch for rainclouds. Rain produces grass to fatten the cattle, and crops that spell the difference between prosperity and hard times. Rain is nearly always welcome during the spring, summer and fall.

The climate is not really harsh. Temperatures range from an average of 73 degrees in summer to 15 degrees in winter. Extreme temperatures from 115 degrees above to 30 degrees below zero may be registered in parts of the state, but such heat and cold are both unusual and of short duration.

Lack of rain, hostile Indians and transportation problems kept settlers out of South Dakota for a long time. The Great American Desert myth did not fade until the 1860's, when returning soldiers came to the eastern part of Dakota as homesteaders. Dakota Territory, including what is now North and South Dakota, was established in 1861.

The West-river area remained in control of the Indians until Custer's expedition of 1874 discovered gold in the Black Hills. When the news got back to the East, thousands of men converged on the gold rush towns of Deadwood, Lead, and Crook City. Cattlemen moved into the west on the heels of the gold seekers, as soon as federal troops had subdued the Indians.

These very different groups of people created the state that exists today: homesteaders in the east, gold miners and cattlemen in the west.

So the differences between the three major parts of South Dakota are not just a matter of geography, though the natural setting is an important factor. Each section of the state has its own way of life, its own people and traditions.

Chapter 3

Pheasant and Farms

The East-river, or Prairie Plains, is a land of pheasants, farms, and a palace made of corn.

Mitchell is much like any small midwestern town: quiet, friendly, a shopping center for farmers in the area, with parks, a museum, a private college. But Mitchell has one thing that no other American town has: a corn palace.

The palace is actually made of wood. But each year, early in the fall, the outside of the building is completely covered with pictures and designs made of corn and outlined with grains and grasses. Oscar Howe, a nationally famous artist and full-blooded Dakota Indian, creates the pictures.

The original Mitchell Corn Palace was built in 1892. It was rebuilt in 1905, and the present structure was constructed in 1921. The palace is about half a block square and is used as a civic arena for

Mitchell Corn Palace

the town. Basketball games, dances, stage shows, conventions and exhibits are held in the Corn Palace throughout the year. Each September name bands and entertainers appear in the Corn Palace Festival, which draws visitors from all over the Midwest.

Corn is appropriate material for a palace in eastern South Dakota. For corn is the basic crop of the farms in the area: corn for sale and for fattening the thousands of cattle and hogs produced each year.

Most of the land in the Prairie Plains area of South Dakota is level. It takes three weeks for water to run through the James River from the North Dakota border to the Nebraska border. This level farmland makes it possible for complicated machinery to increase yields for farmers.

The mechanical corn pickers, combines, hay balers and other machines help each man to cultivate more and more land. This means that farms in South Dakota are getting larger. Not as many people are needed to maintain the farms, so the population is shifting from rural areas to larger towns and cities. Communities like Sioux Falls, Yankton, Huron, Watertown and Aberdeen are growing in size while many smaller towns and rural areas have fewer residents each year.

In spite of the shifting population, the eastern part of South Dakota is still a farming region. And though corn is the basic crop there are other cash crops that thrive in the hot, dry summers. South Dakota leads the nation in the production of "Kentucky" bluegrass seed! Other important crops are alfalfa, wheat, rye, sorghum and wild hay.

South Dakota farmers always face one major problem: water. But in the eastern part of the state rainfall is usually adequate. When it is not, farmers tighten their belts and wait for another year.

When homesteaders began to move into Dakota Territory in the 1860's they found a tantalizingly rich soil which lacked only a little more rain to ensure bumper crops. Eastern South Dakota was a wide, treeless land of wild grass or "prairie hay" when the first settlers came. With little or no wood to use as building material, they cut bricks from the tough prairie sod to make their houses.

In addition to the lack of rain, early homesteaders in South Dakota had to contend with fierce blizzards in winter, heat waves in summer, and periodic raids on the crops by clouds of grasshoppers. The hoppers would come in July, often so thick that their flight blotted out the sun. They would light on a field of ripening wheat or corn and stay for six or eight days, eating crops, clothes hanging on the line, even fence posts. In 1874 the corn crop was completely destroyed from Yankton to Sioux City by grasshoppers, and not a bushel was gathered for 60 miles.

An unknown homesteader summed up the trials of early-day Dakota farmers in a song set to the tune of "Beulah Land":

> We've reached the land of desert sweet,
> Where nothing grows for man to eat;
> The wind it blows with feverish heat
> Across the plains so hard to beat.
> O Dakota land, sweet Dakota land,
> As on thy fiery soil I stand,
> I look across thy plains
> And wonder why it never rains. . . .
> We have no wheat, we have no oats,
> We have no corn to feed our shoats;
> We do not live, we only stay;
> We are too poor to get away.

In spite of all the hardships, many farmers did stay, and the "fiery plains" of South Dakota began to produce an abundance of corn, wheat, oats and hay. The building of railroads brought more settlers and allowed farmers to transport their products to distant markets.

Another trial for the farmers of eastern South Dakota came in the 1930's. The whole country was plunged into a financial depression during those years, and at the same time South Dakota experienced a series of severe droughts. Clouds of dust blew across the open plains in the "dirty thirties" and the grasshoppers came back to eat what crops there were. Many farmers lost their land through mortgage foreclosures, and more than half the state's banks failed.

Still, some of the Dakota farmers hung on until the worst was over. Soil conservation came into practice, shelter belts of trees were planted, and gradually the farms began to produce well again.

Farm life in South Dakota has changed a great deal since the homesteading days. Nearly all farmhouses have electricity, running water, and other modern conveniences. Farmers today must be highly skilled in the use of complex machinery and have a wealth of scientific information as well. Many go to South Dakota State University at Brookings or to other colleges to learn about livestock and farm management, conservation and related subjects.

Today two-thirds of the farm income in South Dakota comes from livestock. A common business in eastern South Dakota is the operation of large feedlots, where cattle are brought in to be fattened before being sold to meat packers.

There is one other "crop" which receives a great deal of attention in the East-river area, and that is the pheasant.

Harvesters at work

On the south edge of Sioux Falls is a weather-beaten old building standing near the edge of the Big Sioux River. This is Hazelville, where Dr. A. Zetlitz imported the first Chinese ringneck pheasants to South Dakota.

Dr. Zetlitz was a character whose neighbors sometimes wondered at the strange birds he kept at his estate. Hungarian partridge, peacocks, wood ducks and other unusual wildlife at one time shared the woods around Hazelville with the pheasants.

In 1898 Dr. Zetlitz brought two roosters and four hen pheasants to his estate. He managed to raise about two dozen chicks in the next few months, and some were released around Sioux Falls.

It was 1908 before the pheasants got a real start in South Dakota. Private citizens released some pheasants around Redfield that year. In 1911 the Game, Fish and Parks Department of South Dakota released 48 pairs of birds. Between 1914 and 1917 some 7,000 more were added. By the mid-forties it was estimated that there were 16,000,000 pheasants in South Dakota.

The male pheasant is as beautiful as any bird in the world, with his blue-green head, red wattles, white ring around the neck, and multicolored tail. There are pheasants in other states, but none comes close to the number of birds to be found in South Dakota.

A typical pheasant hunt might start around noon at the edge of a cornfield near Howard, in the James River valley of eastern South Dakota. The land is flat; the bright blue sky spreads unbroken by clouds for miles in all directions. It is a crisp, fall day, and the hunters wear jackets and bright red hats.

"Let's get started," says an experienced hunter at one end of the field, and the party begins walking through the field. The dry cornstalks are taller than a man's head, and the hunters lose sight of each other, but they stay together by listening to footsteps. The only other sound is the rustling of the dry corn leaves.

"There they go!" someone shouts.

There is a flapping noise, and six cock pheasants rise out of the corn, flying low. Guns crack, two of the pheasants fall, and the others disappear into another field across the road.

Some 3,000,000 male pheasants are killed by hunters in South

29

Dakota during a good year. This has little or no effect on the total number of pheasants in the state. Numbers are limited by food supply and by the amount of nesting area—uncultivated land where eggs can be hatched without being disturbed.

Pheasants are not hunted merely for sport, for the birds make excellent eating. Hunting the birds provides an opportunity for exercise, fresh air and excitement. This may be why the little airport in a town like Howard is crowded during the hunting season with private planes from all over the United States.

Many rifle clubs in South Dakota offer courses in gun use and hunting safety for boys who are ready to go after pheasants for the first time. The moment when a twelve-year-old gets his wings was described by a South Dakota mother this way:

> I want to see the proud grin on his face the day he brings home his first pheasant, and I am going to cook it and force some of it down if it's as old as Solomon because I remember the day my kid brother got his first one. He carried that pheasant into the house like a badge of honor, and when he handed it to my mother his eyes weren't a kid's any more. Every boy deserves that moment. When he is older, the amount of meat on the table will depend more on his take-home pay than on his marksmanship. But that first time, he knows what it is to be a provider. He knows it is a proud thing.

Pheasants range throughout South Dakota, with heaviest concentration in the east-central part of the state. Here, particularly along the James River, a traveler might easily see twenty pheasants in an hour's drive.

The James, or "Jim," River, a tributary of the Missouri, runs through the heart of the Prairie Plains. Within its valley is the richest farmland in South Dakota. The towns of Aberdeen, Redfield, Huron, Mitchell and Yankton serve as centers for business and education in the rural areas of the Jim River valley. Each of these towns has its own personality, from Aberdeen with its famous Fischer quintuplets to Yankton, the oldest of the South Dakota towns and once capital of Dakota Territory—but all base their economy and way of life on the fertile farms around them.

The northeastern corner of South Dakota is distinctly different. French explorers called it Coteau des Prairies, hills of the prairies. The rolling land is dotted with natural lakes, and its altitude is considerably higher than that of the James River valley.

The soil in the northeast is rich but rocky. In an area of about 30 square miles around Milbank, South Dakota, is one of the best deposits of granite in the United States. Six granite quarries around Milbank produce 30 percent of the dressed monumental granite quarried in this country each year. The stone has a rich, dark color and is exceptionally strong and long-lasting.

Milbank is also the birthplace of the now nationwide American Legion Junior Baseball program. There members of the South Dakota Department of the Legion first proposed the idea of sponsoring summer baseball competition for youth in 1925.

The lakes in the Coteau des Prairies are small in comparison to the man-made lakes on the Missouri, but they have their own beauty. Many of them recall the days when this was Indian territory: Enemy Swim Lake, Blue Dog Lake, Punished Woman's Lake. Fort Sisseton, still standing in the heart of the lake country, was built at the time of the Indian outbreaks of 1864.

Southeastern South Dakota centers on Sioux Falls, the largest city in the state. Named for the falls of the Big Sioux River nearby, the community is busy with retail trade, meat-packing, manufacturing, and education.

Most of the major state institutions of South Dakota are located in the populous southeastern section. The School for the Deaf, Crippled Children's School, State Penitentiary, and Children's Home are all in Sioux Falls. Redfield is the site of the state home for the mentally retarded, and the main facility for psychiatric care is the Yankton State Hospital.

Sioux Falls also serves as a cultural center for eastern South Dakota. Its symphony orchestra, art exhibits, concert series and dramatic productions attract not only Sioux Falls residents but many people from surrounding towns and rural areas.

31

Ring-necked pheasants

Horizons dominate South Dakota. In the east, they are broken by towns, shelter belts of trees, a few small hills. Occasionally there is a more unusual sight against the sky. Two of these, the Spirit Mound and the Atomic Power Plant, lie within a few miles of each other in the Sioux Falls area and illustrate the past and future of South Dakota.

The Spirit Mound north of Vermillion was built some time between A.D. 500 and 1000 by the mysterious Mound Builders who inhabited the Midwest before the better-known Indian tribes of the last several hundred years moved in. Eastern South Dakota has many of these mounds still in existence. Archeologists say that the builders buried their dead in the mounds, with almost as much elaborate care as the Egyptians used in their pyramids.

Studies of the contents of these mounds have taught us much about the lives of the builders. They tilled the earth with hoes made of stone, smoked tobacco in carved pipes, and liked to paint their bodies with red ochre. No one knows for certain what happened to the Mound Builders, but they are a part of the earliest human heritage of eastern South Dakota.

The Pathfinder Atomic Power Plant makes a different silhouette against the horizon. It has the sharp, functional lines of modern science; it is the shape of the future.

The plant was named in honor of John C. Frémont, the explorer who was known as Pathfinder by the Dakota Indians he met in 1838. Begun in 1959, the project was undertaken by Northern States Power Company with research and development assistance from the Atomic Energy Commission. Nine other power companies took part in the development of the plant and will benefit from its research and training facilities.

Pathfinder is the nation's first all-atomic electric generating plant. It was built at a cost of $34,000,000 to promote knowledge of peaceful uses of atomic energy. Nuclear energy is used to produce steam and superheat it. The steam, heated by a controlled atomic reaction of enriched uranium fuel, reaches a temperature of 825 degrees before entering the turbogenerator.

The electricity produced by this process seems no different from

34

conventional power to the users in the Sioux Falls area. When the Pathfinder plant was built, it was more expensive to generate electricity using atomic fuel. This has changed, however, and modern atomic plants now produce power at less cost than plants using conventional fuels.

Engineers at the Pathfinder Atomic Power Plant are developing ways of bringing down the cost of atomically generated electricity. Supplies of coal and oil are dwindling in the United States. Research such as that being carried on at the Pathfinder plant may provide a new source of power for future Americans.

An ancient mound and an atomic power plant—both part of the land of contrasts that is South Dakota.

In the central part of the state, the horizon seems to widen. There is more distance between farms and between towns; then the farms give way to grazing land. Moving through this part of South Dakota is almost like being on an ocean, especially in the dim light of dusk or dawn. Gently waving grass stretches in all directions. When the sun goes down and darkness moves in, the great landscape vanishes. A light or two in a distant house can be seen for miles, making the prairie all the more lonely. A silence never heard in cities hangs over the open land.

Driving through this sort of country from the busy East-river, a traveler comes suddenly upon Pierre. The capital city of South Dakota is set in majestic isolation on the banks of the transformed Missouri River, belonging to neither east nor west. No matter how carefully marked maps are followed, it is a surprise to see the dome of the capitol building rising over Pierre.

Lying as it does between the major parts of South Dakota, Pierre also contains elements of the old and the new. Lewis and Clark camped near this spot and met with Arikara Indians who once built permanent villages on the banks of the Missouri. Fort Pierre, just across the river, was once one of the busiest fur-trading posts in North America. The Vérendrye brothers, French fur traders, buried a metal plate near Fort Pierre in 1743 which claimed the entire area for France.

The new is present at South Dakota's capital city, too. Nearby is

Oahe Dam with its complex power plants. The dam represents the skill of modern engineering; its inland lake reveals the potential of a state that was once part of the Great American Desert.

Today plans are being made to utilize some of the water provided

by the Missouri River dams to irrigate a half million acres of farmland in the Jim River valley. Thus the Prairie Plains of South Dakota may lose their dependence on the whims of the weather.

West of Pierre lies the second part of the state: the Great Plains.

South Dakota farmlands

Chapter 4

Cattle Country

It is 6:30 A.M., and the sun is rising high and warm over the range in Butte County, western South Dakota. Twenty men in blue jeans, western shirts and hats finish the last of a breakfast cooked over an open fire and proceed with morning's work: branding nearly 300 calves.

Branding irons are heated over a fire made of old fence posts. As the hours pass each calf is roped, thrown to the ground, branded and vaccinated. It is hard, hot work.

Modern-day ranchers lead a life not too different from that of the cowboys of western movies, at least in the work they do. Today the branding irons might be heated with butane gas, or they might even be supercooled in dry ice for the new freeze-branding method. Vaccinations for blackleg, malignant edema and hemorrhagic septicemia were introduced by modern science not so long ago. But cattle must still be herded and roped, and the horse is as essential as ever.

Cattle grazing on a South Dakota prairie

A rancher's brand is a very important possession, and each one is registered in the state capital. The brand not only identifies the owner of a calf but also represents that owner's reputation as a cattleman.

Probably no tradition in South Dakota is so firmly rooted as that of the cattle industry. The lifeblood of the state's economy is still, and always has been, livestock. And the ranchers of western South Dakota are more than reminders of a former way of life; they are vital, active, and as much a part of the future as the past.

There was a time, in the days of the open range, when a man could ride on horseback throughout the western half of South Dakota without seeing a fence. Texas longhorns moved into Dakota Territory when the Black Hills were opened to white men during the gold rush. Cattlemen were attracted to the area by the highly nutritious, "belly-high" prairie grass which covered the rolling land. The long-horns did well in the hot, dry summers and found shelter through the winters in the coulees and breaks which are so common in the Great Plains.

By 1884 there were nearly 800,000 cattle in western South Dakota. The ranchers did not have to own their land, and almost anyone could start a herd with a horse or two and a few head of cattle.

The cattle did not have the land to themselves. Coyotes, prairie dogs and herds of wild horses were common. Rattlesnakes slithered through the tall grass. There were deer and antelope and terrible gray wolves. These wolves were the most serious threat to the lives of the cattle. Sometimes weighing as much as 100 pounds, they would kill calves and colts in spite of the most careful guarding.

And in the beginning, there were the buffalo or bison. A single herd of wild buffalo took five days to pass the camp of Colonel Dodge in 1871. The huge, humpbacked animals covered an area 25 miles wide and 50 miles long, and estimates judge this one herd to have included 4,000,000 buffalo.

Indians hunted only as many of these animals as they needed, but the white men were not so careful. A good buffalo hunter with a Sharp's rifle could kill a hundred in an hour. At first the pelts had some value, but then they became too common and were sold for a few cents each. Some buffalo were shot just for the tongue meat, and the rest of the carcass was left to rot. The Dakotas were soon covered with bleached bones. By 1889 there were less than a hundred wild buffalo left in the United States and cattle had taken over the Great Plains.

In fact, the American bison very nearly became extinct before the turn of the century. But today there is a large herd of buffalo in South Dakota's Custer State Park, and tourists can eat buffalo steak in many of the state's restaurants.

Ironically, it was a cattleman who did much to save the buffalo from extinction. "Scotty" Philip was one of the most successful early ranchers in South Dakota, and it was his carefully reared herd of more than 900 buffalo that ensured the comeback of the unusual animals.

Philip came to the United States from Scotland at the age of sixteen. He punched cattle for a while in Wyoming, prospected for gold in the Black Hills, and got his start as a rancher in 1881. By 1900 he had a big spread, the 73 Ranch, near Fort Pierre.

Scotty Philip had many friends among the Indians. His wife was part Cheyenne. He understood their sorrow in seeing the buffalo, their traditional source of food, killed off. In 1899 Philip bought a small herd of buffalo from the administrators of the Peter Dupree estate. He fenced in 3,500 acres along the Missouri, and within a few years had developed a thriving herd.

Though his preservation of the buffalo was important, Scotty Philip was first and foremost a cattleman, and western South Dakota was cattle country. For a time it looked as though that might be changed.

In the late 1880's, just when the cattle industry was having its greatest success, homesteaders began moving into the West-river country with the railroad. "Honyockers" they were called by the cowboys. They built houses, put up fences, planted crops. There were clashes between farmers and ranchers, but barbed wire had come to stay. By 1900 the open range was gone.

Even so, the homesteaders soon learned that the soil which grew lush grass for cattle would not yield enough crops to support them

Buffalo

very long. Corn burned or was eaten by grasshoppers. The home-steaders who managed to hang on to their land turned more and more to cattle raising.

So the Great Plains area of South Dakota remained grazing land. The tough Texas longhorns were gradually displaced by shorthorns, Herefords, Black Angus, Scottish Highlanders. Ranchers built permanent homes, raised hay for winter feed for the cattle, constructed corrals. The cattle industry was now big business.

The ranchers and their animals suffered at least as much as East-river farmers during the "dirty thirties." Dust clouds blotted out the sun. The grass died; the earth was scorched and cracked. Home-steaders in their futile attempts to till the land had broken the sod and killed much of the deep-rooted prairie grass; now there was nothing to hold the soil. Cattle died by the thousands, and land was lost for taxes. Sand and tumbleweed made the area look like the Great American Desert of its former reputation.

But the worst was finally over. In the years since World War II the ranches of the West-river have been rebuilt, and South Dakota is still one of the nation's leaders in the raising of livestock.

The cattlemen use pickup trucks as well as horses, now. The big cattle drives belong to the past; animals are taken to market in stock trucks. Small airplanes may be used to drop food to cattle stranded in blizzards.

Airplanes are important to a very special ranch near Buffalo in northwestern South Dakota. Sky Ranch for boys was founded in 1960 by Father Don Murray, a priest with a special interest in flying, ranching and problem youngsters.

Boys from all over the country live in the new three-story dormitory at the ranch. They have different racial and religious backgrounds; some come from broken homes; some have a background of trouble with the law. The "wide open spaces" of the Great Plains are strange to many from city slums. On the 3,000-acre ranch they learn to handle livestock—and to fly.

From the beginning Father Murray has included flying lessons in his program. The skill and adventure gained in this way are pluses added to more conventional education.

Other South Dakota youngsters and adults find excitement in a truly western sport—rodeo.

Throughout every summer West-river towns have their rodeos— from small, local contests to national events. Unlike athletes in some other sports, rodeo cowboys have no assured salaries. They compete for prize money, risking serious injury in the process.

The bull riding event is a good example of the dangers of rodeo. Top cowboys may be able to stay on only half the bulls they ride until the eight-second whistle. The bulls, usually part Brahma, are fast-moving and vicious. Since they will attack horses, no pickup men can be used to rescue a cowboy who has been thrown.

The contestant uses a rope which has been looped around the bull's middle. There is a handhold on the rope shaped something like a duffle bag handle. When a cowboy is about to ride a bull, he gets on the animal in a chute on the edge of the rodeo ring. He wears a glove on the hand with which he will hang on, to prevent rope burns. The slack on the rope is taken up and the free end wound around the rider's hand to give a better grip. Then the cowboy nods, the gate is opened, and the bull plunges out into the ring.

The next few seconds tell the story. The bull bucks and twists across the ring, the man on his back trying desperately to hang on. Sometimes he does stay mounted until the eight-second whistle blows, and then he may be in the money. But many times the rider is flung to the ground and faced by an enraged, sharp-horned animal weighing about a ton. If he is able, the man then races for the fence on the edge of the ring.

Sometimes, a rider thrown by a bull is stunned or crippled by broken bones. Sometimes his hand is caught in the handhold, and he is dragged helplessly around the ring. At such moments the rodeo clowns prove their courage.

Clowns have a much more important function in rodeo than simply making people laugh. When a man has been hurt they distract the bull's attention with their antics, and often help an injured cowboy get to safety.

Bull riding is only one of many rodeo events that are popular in western South Dakota. Bareback riding, roping, steer wrestling,

Young rider from Sky Ranch

saddle bronc riding and other contests keep this sport fast-moving and varied. Rodeo pits man against animal in a struggle of muscle, bone, coordination and grit. It suits the inhabitants of a land where men and animals have been together from the beginning, and where skill and courage have always been prized.

Western South Dakota had its gunmen, like other parts of the Great Plains. Some are still famous; many have been forgotten. But it was not the badmen who built the region. The working cattlemen despised the robbers and killers of the old West.

Today, as in the past, the ranchers consider themselves builders. Their cattle help to feed the nation, and their use of the land preserves it for the future.

Life in the ranch country of western South Dakota seems almost untouched by the urbanization of the rest of the United States. There are towns: Murdo, Philip, Faith, Winner, Belle Fourche,

45

Bison, Timber Lake—but these are small and separated by hundreds of miles of nearly open land. Ranches are large, and neighbors distant.

In the area there are some signs of the twentieth century, too. Power lines cross the plains on their high towers. Commercial airliners fly overhead on their way from Denver to Minneapolis. And occasionally, beside a lonely road, is a small area surrounded by a high fence.

These are the Minuteman installations, part of America's most sophisticated defense program. Buried beneath the ground in this lonely range country are missiles which could be used in the event of a nuclear attack.

A hundred and fifty Minuteman Intercontinental Ballistic Missiles are kept in readiness at fifteen sites, with each site supervised by carefully trained two-man crews. These men are attached to nearby Ellsworth Air Force Base.

Stockyards

But not even modern missile sites can alter the look of the western plains, or the fact that this is cattle country. The people who live in the West-river area are mostly ranchers, and their lives and activities center on raising and selling cattle.

A typical ranch is that of Mr. and Mrs. Harold Coe, 16 miles north of Belle Fourche in Butte County. Some 350 Hereford cows graze on the 14,000-acre ranch.

The year's crop of calves, born in April and May, is rounded up for branding early in June. On the appointed day, men from neighboring ranches come to help; and starting on horseback from the distant corners of the Coe land, they herd the cattle to the central corrals.

There the calves are roped, tied, vaccinated, and branded with the "heart-tail" brand of the ranch. The job is finished by noon, and families from the eight nearby ranches come for a big neighborhood meal. Roundups in South Dakota provide a social time as well as a chance to get help with an important job, and this can mean much in a land of long distances and few people.

"I don't feel isolated," says Mrs. Coe. "I come to town at least every two or three days. We have all the modern conveniences in our home, and a good road."

Automobiles, radios, television sets and telephones have eliminated the isolation of the old days.

Education is still a problem of distance. One-room schools used to serve the needs of rural South Dakota, but the course offerings of such schools are limited and it is hard to find qualified teachers. The trend today is for reorganization into larger school districts with centrally located facilities. This means that South Dakota youngsters may travel many miles to school, sometimes in winter starting out before dawn and getting home after dark.

Modern ranchers face other problems. It is getting increasingly difficult for individual ranchers who work their own land to compete with large corporations, often from out of the state, who buy up land and hire people to tend their cattle. The cost of land and equipment is constantly going up, while the price of beef holds steady or drops.

48

Today, a rancher needs a variety of expensive equipment to raise good beef cattle. Harold Coe owns a pickup truck, a large stock truck, two tractors, hay baling equipment, and many tools. He also keeps ten horses. Cattle must be vaccinated against a number of diseases and fed vitamins and food supplements.

These supplements are given mainly when the cows are ready to have their new calves. The native range grass is remarkably rich and nourishing. Because it has little moisture content, freezing does not seem to affect its quality, and cattle thrive on it the year around. The same grass is cut and made into hay in the summertime to be fed to the cattle when deep snows cover their winter pastures.

In the fall, animals ready for market are sold to feedlots in the eastern part of the state to be fattened for slaughter. The rest of the herd stays through the winter, the new calves are born, and the cycle starts all over again.

Life on a South Dakota ranch would not appeal to everyone. Profits are uncertain, work is often hot and dirty, and it can be lonely. But to the cattlemen it offers independence, a chance to live and work in the out-of-doors, privacy, freedom from routine. In the quiet of the Great Plains a man can learn to be alone with his thoughts. He can appreciate the beauty around him and feel his close ties with earth, weather, animals and birds.

Western South Dakota also provides a setting in which people of the twentieth century can sense the long ages that went into the making of the earth as it is today. Nowhere is this more true than in the barren, mysterious Badlands.

Chapter 5

Fossils, Cliffs and Caves

Sabertooth tigers once hunted here. Three-toed horses, ancestors of the camel, and prehistoric rhinoceroses have left their marks. There were large turtles, ancient forms of the alligator, entelodonts (large piglike animals) and titanotheres.

The Badlands of western South Dakota are one of the nation's richest fossil beds, and were formed some 25,000,000 to 40,000,000 years ago. The weird, otherworldly look of the place makes it easy to believe that this is true. Rocky spires marked with bands of color tell the story. Each band or layer is another chapter. By studying these formations, geologists can determine much about the past.

The Badlands landscape as we know it today probably did not begin to form until about 1,000,000 years ago. Fossils found there are the remains of animals buried in flooding streams. The process of erosion carved out of the face of the earth the strange and beautiful

South Dakota Badlands

Indian petroglyphs on sandstone, Custer National Forest

formations which can be seen today. Streams cut new channels through the soft rock, and occasional downpours of rain continued the natural sculpture.

Now pronghorn antelope, bison, deer, coyotes, bobcats and chipmunks are found where once the prehistoric beasts lived and died. A hike along the Badlands fossil trail gives a good view of the relics of some of these animals, covered and protected by plastic skylight domes.

When the first French-Canadian trappers came to Dakota, they named this area *les mauvaises terres à traverser,* bad lands to travel across. And the Indians had a similar name: *mako sica,* bad land.

Studies indicate that Indian hunters camped in the Badlands 900 years ago. The cliffs and blind canyons would have been ideal for the trapping and killing of buffalo.

Later, the Sioux became dominant in South Dakota. They had their own idea of the origin of the Badlands. According to a Sioux legend, the Badlands were formed by an angry medicine man who placed a curse on the land.

When Chief Big Foot was trying to escape the cavalry during the Ghost Dance movement of 1890, he led them through a pass in the Badlands which still bears his name.

Badlands National Monument covers 174 square miles of land in western South Dakota. The exposed rocks which make up the peaks of the Badlands are composed of clay, mudstone and sandstone. These relatively soft rocks are still changing form through the effects of wind and weather. Each year new fossils are revealed by the constant erosion of the rock.

At first glance the Badlands seem completely barren. But there is life among the rocks and spires. In some places wildflowers live: phlox, vetch, mariposa lily, and others. Yucca or Spanish bayonet with its sharp-pointed leaves blooms late in June.

But all living things are dwarfed by the miles of jagged rock. Visitors may be reminded of pictures of the moon's surface. You might almost expect a creature from another world to step out from behind one of the formations—or a saber-tooth tiger.

The Badlands have been the object of scientific study for many years. In 1852 Dr. David Owen, who worked as a geologist for the General Land Office, wrote a report of fossil collections from the Badlands. The "Owen Report" is considered by many scientists as the beginning of the study of vertebrate paleontology in this country.

A person does not have to be trained in science to sense the millions of years of natural history recorded in the corridors and canyons of the Badlands. Anyone with a little imagination can feel the incredible age of the place.

Similar experiences can be had in other parts of western South Dakota. Less famous than the Badlands National Monument, but equally fascinating, is Custer National Forest in the northwestern part of the state.

Ranchers call this rugged country the "jumping-off-spot." The Cave Hills section of the forest once served as a popular hiding place for outlaws. Ludlow Cave, the largest of the caves, sheltered many a western bandit in the early days of Dakota Territory.

Pronghorn buck

Scratched in the sandstone walls of the cave are Indian petroglyphs, prehistoric drawings depicting animals, symbols and magical rites. Experts say that this is not Sioux art, but the work of some earlier tribes. It has even been suggested that Pueblos from the Southwest might have visited the area at one time.

The Cave Hills are large cliffs which once had limestone caps. The tops of these cliffs are now covered with pines. South of the Cave Hills are the Short Pines, where smaller hills and deep gorges dominate the countryside.

Uranium mines and oil wells may be seen among the hills. But Custer National Forest, like the Badlands, is also a happy hunting ground for seekers of fossils. The town of Bison, 30 miles to the east, has a nationally famous museum containing many fossils. A team from the South Dakota School of Mines and Technology found a nearly perfect fossilized head of Triceratops, the "frilled" dinosaur, in the limestone formations of Custer National Forest. Remains of huge turtles, tigers and cephalopods (sea mollusks) indicate that this was once a warm, wet land, more a jungle than a forest.

The Slim Buttes section of the Custer National Forest covers more than 40 miles south and east of the Cave Hills and Short Pines. Here are towering cliffs of limestone split by spectacular canyons.

Nearby is the Slim Buttes battlefield, where Sioux veterans of the Custer fight were overtaken by the U.S. Cavalry. Several hundred of the Indians were surprised by the soldiers at sunrise September 9, 1876. Taking shelter high in the hills behind the limestone outcroppings, the Indians were able to hold off their attackers and escaped during the night.

Petrified trees and logs may be found in many parts of western South Dakota. A large collection of specimens is kept at the Petrified Wood Park at Lemmon. Buried under a hill between Reva and Bison was found what may be the largest petrified tree in existence, more than 75 feet high.

In and around the Custer National Forest can be seen many of the 30,000 wild pronghorn antelope that live in South Dakota. The pronghorns are actually not antelope. They are a unique American animal with no relatives anywhere in the world. They are swift and graceful, with eyesight so keen it equals that of a man using eight-power binoculars. The males have forked, hollow horns.

The pronghorns' grazing lands are relatively undisturbed by man. Population in the jumping-off-spot is only two people per square mile. There are some ranchers and sheepherders in this country of buttes and rimrock and grassy plains, but their homes are few and far between.

Along the western border of South Dakota the open plains, buttes and badlands give way to the granite fortress known as Paha Sapa, the Black Hills.

Chapter 6

Paha Sapa

Millions of years ago, in the same upheaval that produced the Rocky Mountains, South Dakota's Black Hills were thrust up out of the earth. The Himalayas were still marshland, then, and the Alps had not been formed.

The Black Hills are really neither black nor hills. Their dark green color comes from the acres of ponderosa pine and spruce trees which cover most of the surfaces. And they are full-fledged mountains, with Harney Peak, at more than 7,000 feet above sea level, the highest point between the Rockies and the Alps.

Black Hills is a translation of the Sioux name for the mountains, Paha Spa. A more accurate rendering would be Hills of the Shadows. Before the white men came, the Indians regarded the Black Hills as sacred, a dwelling place of gods.

It is not hard to see why they thought so. The granite peaks, still blue lakes and deep forests are as awe-inspiring today as they must

Bighorn sheep

have been when Sioux boys came alone to Paha Sapa to fast and see visions.

Today several million tourists visit the Black Hills every summer. They come from all over the United States and the world, many to camp high in the hills.

But with the fall most of the visitors leave the Black Hills to the South Dakotans. Many of the people who live in the hills are descendants of the miners who came here seeking gold in 1876. Others are drawn by the beauty of the area, and the climate.

The Black Hills region is usually the warmest part of South Dakota in winter, the coolest in summer. Many winter days provide shirt-sleeve weather, and some enthusiasts even refer to the Black Hills as the Banana Belt of the state.

There are two reasons for the markedly different weather in the hills. Cold air masses tend to seek low elevations, and so often bypass the hills. And warm chinook winds may blow into the Black Hills during the winter months, melting snow and raising temperatures.

Black Hills weather is quite unpredictable because of these factors. On January 22, 1943, the temperature in Rapid City fluctuated between a low of 5 degrees above zero and a high of 60. The thermometer went up and down like a Yo-yo, climbing or dropping as much as 30 degrees in five minutes.

Men on one side of the Sheraton-Johnson Hotel basked in the sun in shirt sleeves; a block away on the other side of the hotel people shivered in overcoats. A few minutes later there was a complete reversal. People bundled up, then took their wraps off, put them on again. Traffic was stalled by windshields suddenly frosting over. This particular day in Rapid City was known as "the chinook to end all chinooks."

Weathermen had an explanation. A cold air mass had kept temperatures below zero for weeks. Above this cold air hovered a layer of warm air, almost motionless. When the wind came up it blew gusts of the warm air down into the city, changing direction now and then, and creating the freakish weather.

Black Hills residents think of the mountains as divided into two parts: the Northern Hills and the Southern Hills. The Southern

Hills area includes the towns that cluster around Rapid City and Custer, while the Northern Hills centers in Lead, Deadwood, Sturgis and Spearfish.

Of the larger Black Hills towns, only Lead and Deadwood are actually in the hills. The others were built in valleys along the edges of the mountains, where there was more space available.

Rapid City is the trade center of the hills, and of most of western South Dakota. Founded during the gold rush, it grew from a population of 13,000 in 1940 to 42,000 in 1960. Much of this growth resulted from the location of Ellsworth Air Force Base nearby.

Visitors to Rapid City are sometimes startled to glance up and see a huge beast standing on a hilltop above the city. This 70-foot-long model of a brontosaurus is one of seven life-size prehistoric animals constructed by Emmet A. Sullivan in Rapid City's Dinosaur Park. Made of concrete, the statues represent creatures which once lived in western South Dakota. The bones and fossils of such animals are displayed in the Museum of Geology in Rapid City.

Custer, not far from Rapid City, is notable for its extremely wide main street. The street was built that way so that the supply-carrying bull trains of gold rush days could turn around in the street. Since these trains sometimes consisted of as many as 60 wagons and 400 head of oxen, it is easy to see why the street is so wide.

Nearby is Custer State Park, one of the largest state parks in the country. Many animals live there: deer, elk, mountain sheep, white mountain goats, wild donkeys, and more than 1,000 buffalo.

People driving through the park can see the great, shaggy animals grazing near the road or wandering across it. The herd is now so well established that the South Dakota State Park Service holds an annual auction of live buffalo to keep the numbers at a manageable level. Rich, juicy buffalo meat is served in many Black Hills restaurants.

The Custer State Park buffalo, along with Mount Rushmore and South Dakotan Ben Black Elk, were featured in the first international Telstar broadcast in 1962.

The Needles Highway with its tunnels and "pigtail bridges" is another favorite of tourists and natives alike. The highway winds

Calamity Jane   Poker Alice

through miles and miles of sharp rocky spires and spectacular views.

The University of South Dakota operates a summer theater in Custer State Park. The Black Hills Playhouse presents drama and musical comedy throughout each summer.

At the extreme southern edge of the hills is the town of Hot Springs, named for the warm mineral spring which provides swimming the year around in Evans Plunge. In summer the Battle of the Little Big Horn is reenacted at Hot Springs in the Crazy Horse Pageant.

In the Northern Hills the twin gold rush towns of Deadwood and Lead (pronounced "leed") perch high in the mountains, their narrow, twisting streets and steep hills following the contour of the gulches in which they are built. Deadwood is famous as the onetime home of western characters like Calamity Jane, Wild Bill Hickok, Poker Alice, and Preacher Smith. Twenty thousand people surged into Deadwood Gulch in 1876, when the Black Hills gold rush began.

Deadwood was a wild and woolly town in those days. Gunmen Sam Bass, Wyatt Earp and Bat Masterson came to Deadwood. Murders were common, and there was no real law until the Black Hills were made part of Dakota Territory. Except for the Homestake mine in Lead, gold mining is no longer carried on in the Black Hills. The cost of extracting any large amounts of gold from the rock is too great to make any small operation pay off. Deadwood has not forgotten its past, but its people earn their living in other ways today.

In a fertile valley on the edge of the Northern Hills is Spearfish, a different sort of town. Small farms and ranches have been more important to Spearfish than gold. Black Hills State College is located there, and a large sawmill. But its unique feature is the Black Hills Passion Play.

The story of the Passion Play goes back more than 700 years, to the town of Lünen, Germany. There the monks at the Cappenberg Monastery used to perform the play during Easter Week each year. The roles were later taken by people in the community, who handed them down from generation to generation.

During the 1930's, after Hitler came to power in Germany, the Lünen Passion Play visited the United States. Josef Meier, the seventh of his family to take the leading role of the Christus, brought the company to this country. Because of the situation in Europe and the warm reception the play received here, it was decided not to return to Germany.

In 1938 the touring Passion Play company visited Spearfish. There Josef Meier found a natural amphitheater with perfect acoustics. The mountainous horizon made a beautiful backdrop for an outdoor play. So the ancient European drama located permanently in western South Dakota.

Since that time, millions of people have seen the Black Hills Passion Play. The amphitheater seats 6,500 people; the play is performed three times a week through the summer. In all the years since coming to Spearfish, Josef Meier has never missed a performance.

A core of professional actors assumes most of the speaking roles in the play. Spearfish residents provide the rest of the cast of 200, filling out the crowd scenes, performing as Roman guards, Disciples, merchants, camel drivers and priests. The elaborate set, costumes and lighting add to the impressiveness of the play.

At Sturgis, south of Spearfish, is the newest of South Dakota's state parks. Bear Butte State Park is located on the core of an extinct volcano. The butte was regarded as sacred by several Indian tribes, and was later used as a lookout by army scouts.

In the heart of the Northern Hills, miles of ski trails wind down Terry Peak. South Dakotans and residents of surrounding states come there to try their skills on the Holy Terror, Gold Run, and other trails. A chair lift carries skiers to the top of the ski area and also provides one of the most scenic rides in the Black Hills.

Paha Sapa has more than 1,000,000 acres of ponderosa pine trees, most of them located in the Black Hills National Forest. Lumbering is an important industry in the Black Hills. Timber cutting by sawmills is carefully regulated by the U.S. Forest Service, and new trees are planted to replace what has been cut.

There were about 1,500,000,000 board feet of timber in the Black Hills when the first white men came. Nearly 3,000,000,000 board

The Last Supper from the Black Hills Passion Play

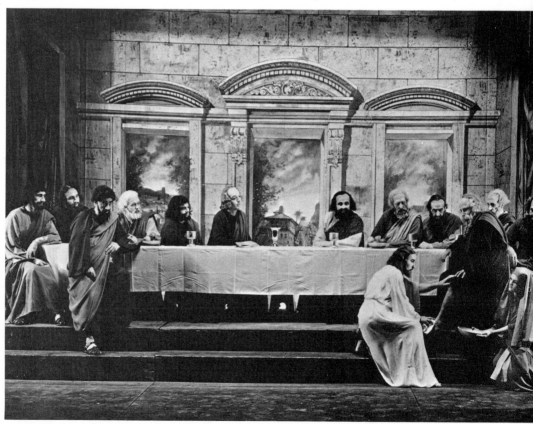

feet have been cut since then, but because of the careful management of the Forest Service there is now more timber than there was before: about 5,000,000,000 board feet .

The ponderosa pine grows tall and very straight, its blue-green needles blending to make the hills look black from a distance. Its lumber is used in many ways: for construction, for posts, pulpwood and poles.

Because the Black Hills are covered with thousands of acres of valuable timber, one of the greatest problems is the danger of fire. When a long siege of hot, dry weather combines with high winds and lightning, or careless people, monster fires may result.

In September of 1959 thousands of volunteers from all over the Black Hills fought a huge forest fire that threatened the town of Deadwood. Many acres of forest were burned, and a column of smoke hung over the town that was visible miles away. Winds up to 45 miles per hour whipped the blaze along a ridge west of Deadwood, and some buildings were burned before the wind changed and the fire fighters got the flames under control.

Deadwood was originally named for the quantities of dead timber around the gulch when the gold seekers came. But its name seems even more appropriate now, for the marks of the 1959 fire still cover the hills around Deadwood. New trees have been planted, but it will be many years before the hillsides are green again.

Fires such as the one near Deadwood are especially dangerous in the Black Hills because of the rugged countryside and the unpredictable winds which may blow through the canyons and gulches.

The Black Hills National Forest contains wildlife as well as trees. Deer are numerous. On a spring evening at dusk it is not uncommon to see forty or fifty of them grazing along the roadside, gracefully leaping fences and disappearing at last into the woods. There are elk, and smaller animals such as beaver, muskrat, porcupines, and squirrels. Wild turkeys strut through the pine forest. Trout swim in the mountain streams.

Back in the hills, away from the large towns and tourist attractions, the forest belongs to the wild things. There are a few signs of man, but the hills look much as they have for centuries.

Here and there is a ghost town or an abandoned gold mine. Castleton, Cacite, Montezuma, Newton City, Tinton: all were founded hopefully in the days of the gold rush; all are now deserted. Tools and mining equipment are rusting; windows are broken, roofs

Lookout tower near Pactola Lake

caving in. The recent craze for weathered boards for building may lead to the end of these ghost towns.

The forest is beautiful and valuable, the scenery superb. But Paha Sapa conceals fabulous treasures beneath its surface, too.

Chapter 7

Under the Hills

The cry "Thar's gold in them thar hills!" has crept into our language, a bit of American folklore which still applies to the Black Hills of South Dakota.

The Homestake gold mine, operating at Lead, is the richest gold mine in the western hemisphere. About $20,000,000 in gold each year is produced at Homestake.

Once there were many other mines in the Black Hills. When white men came here in search of "colors" (gold) in 1876, they staked out scores of mines. Two Johns, Father De Smet, Iron Hill, Hidden Fortune—all were once operating in the Black Hills, named by the whims of gold seekers. W. B. Franklin promised his wife he would name his mine after her if he made a strike. He kept his promise, and called his mine the Holy Terror!

But mining gold was hard work, and as the surface nuggets and

66

Homestake Mining Company's surface plants, Lead, South Dakota

easily reached veins of gold began to play out, many of the smaller mines closed.

Homestake remained. Located in 1876 by two brothers, Moses and Fred Manuel, the Homestake was based on a fabulously rich vein of ore in the hills above Deadwood. The town of Lead grew

up around the original lead or outcropping of ore which led to the Manuels' discovery.

Today Homestake owns some 6,000 acres of mining claims in the Black Hills. Its operations include not only gold mining but uranium, potash, iron, lead and zinc mines in various parts of the world.

Homestake's surface plants, circa 1887

Three hydroelectric plants produce some of the power for the mine. Kirk Power Plant, a coal-burning steam turbine plant, provides the rest.

Modern gold mining is a complicated business. More than a ton of extremely hard ore must be ground up to recover a third of an ounce of gold. Homestake mine shafts now reach down to a depth of nearly 7,000 feet, with about 200 miles of underground passages being worked. In the deepest shafts the temperature is as high as 121 degrees, while near the top it is only 44 degrees.

Miners use air drills and explosives to cut slices of ore about 10 feet into the rock. The broken ore is hoisted to the surface and crushed into half-inch pebbles.

Most of the gold is in such small particles that it cannot even be seen without a microscope. It is removed by two processes. The ore is ground very fine, and quicksilver is added to the grinding mills. About three-fourths of the gold is recovered by its attraction to the quicksilver in a process called amalgamation.

The ore is then soaked in sand vats containing a cyanide solution, which dissolves the gold and carries it out of the bottom of the vats. The gold is removed by adding zinc powder to the cyanide solution and filtering it out.

Through these methods more than 97 percent of the gold in the original ore is recovered. It is refined into small bars of pure gold. These bars weigh 35 pounds, and it takes 3,000,000 pounds of ore to produce one.

All of the Homestake gold is sold to the United States government, and industries obtain what they want to buy from the federal supply. Some of it is used in the manufacture of unique Black Hills gold jewelry. Gold is also needed in such industries as atomic reactors and research, electronics, color photography and dentistry.

In a large chamber a mile below the surface of the earth Homestake crews have helped to establish a project that has nothing to do with gold or mining. It is an atomic testing station which Homestake prepared for use by the Brookhaven National Laboratory of New York.

The station is an experimental one. Its purpose is to detect and study neutrinos from the sun, and thus to learn more about the sun's surface.

Neutrinos are tiny particles which travel at the speed of light and are able to pass through matter—even a mile of granite in the Black Hills! Neutrinos weigh nothing and carry no electrical charge. Four hundred billion of them pass through a square inch of granite every second.

The Brookhaven Laboratory has developed a method of trapping neutrinos in a chemical fluid. But a great volume of this fluid is needed for the experiments, and they must be carried out deep underground so that unwanted cosmic rays are filtered out. The laboratory began looking for a mine that could house a tank with a capacity of 100,000 gallons, and with a mile of rock overhead.

Homestake was chosen for this project in 1964. It took two years for workmen to complete the site. It is now in operation, and the atomic experiments being carried on side by side with gold mining provide one more contrast between old and new in South Dakota.

There is still more under the surface of the Black Hills. Caves honeycomb the hills with underground passages, many of which are still unexplored.

Best known of the Black Hills caves is Wind Cave. It is now a national park. The cave was first discovered in 1881 by an early Black Hills resident named Tom Bingham. While hunting for deer, he noticed a whistling sound coming out of a clump of bushes. Beneath the bushes he found a small opening in the rock, which led to Wind Cave.

There are 10 miles of passages which have been explored in Wind Cave. Visitors can take a guided tour of a little more than a mile through some of the passages which have been electrically lighted. But there remain many more miles which have not been explored. In fact, no one knows just how big Wind Cave really is.

Most of the formations in this limestone cave are called "boxwork"; they look like intricate wood carvings. There are also unusual formations called "frostwork" and "popcorn." All were formed by rainwater seeping through the limestone and dissolving the rock.

71

Modern sand vats at the Homestake Mine

Wind Cave is a natural barometer. When the wind blows out of the cave, the barometer is falling; when the wind blows in, the barometer is rising. The temperature in the cave is always 47 degrees.

Jewel Cave National Monument in the Hell's Canyon area west of Custer is thought to be even larger than Wind Cave.

Herb and Jan Conn, a husband-and-wife spelunking team, have made many explorations in Jewel Cave with the permission of the National Park Service. Their work, with the help of Park Service rangers, has established 24 miles of mapped passages in the cave. But this is probably only a small portion of the total. Wind and barometer studies indicate a volume of something like 4,000,000,000 cubic feet of space in Jewel Cave. "Any way you look at it," say the Conns, "it's a lot of cave!"

Jewel Cave is named for the many formations of calcite crystals, or dogtooth spar, found there. A small portion of the cave is open for tours guided by rangers from the first of June through Labor Day.

Places such as Eerie Boulevard, Rat Hole, Thin Man's Misery, Fourth Dimension, and the Snow Bowl have been found in Jewel Cave and named by the Conns. Helen's Room was named for Helen Gone, a mythical lady invented by the explorers to occupy a remote section of the cave.

In 1962 the Conns found a room beneath a stream bed with silver-colored "balloons" in it. Jan Conn described it as looking "as if somebody had plastered the walls with bubble gum." The National Speleological Society said that nothing like the hydromagnesite balloons had ever been reported to them.

New discoveries are constantly being made as the explorations go on. A tunnel has been dug and an elevator shaft sunk to give easier access to the scenic parts of the cave. The National Park Service is developing the cave so that additional portions of it may be available to the public.

Spelunking is hard work, and it may also be dangerous—especially in a cave as complex as Jewel.

The cave covers four main levels, a maze of interconnecting passages in which explorers could become lost in minutes. Just in the area which has been mapped there are thousands of combinations of routes, most of them branching out into unknown passages. If a person became injured while exploring the cave it could be extremely difficult for rescuers to find him and get him out safely. For this reason exploration is restricted to those persons having sufficient ability and experience.

The Conns have used a system of paper markers when venturing into new parts of the cave, to indicate their route for possible rescuers. They then pick up the markers on their way back.

These journeys have led Herb and Jan Conn to some unique and fascinating discoveries. Early in their work they found the remains of some former expeditions, perhaps by the Michaud brothers who first found the cave in 1900. But in the more remote passages there

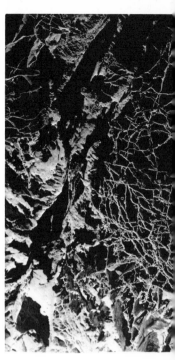

Stalactites, stalagmites, and columns   Boxwork formations

are no such indications, and theirs may be the first human eyes to see the strange formations and "rooms" of Jewel Cave.

The Conns have a mail-order business in hand-carved leather goods, which they make themselves. Herb Conn also helps with the annual maintenance work on the Mount Rushmore National Memorial. But their enthusiasm for the difficult mapping of Jewel Cave continues. Why?

"We'd like to see the cave map continue to grow, and to know what is under the next hill, and the next, and the next. . ."

Both Jewel and Wind Caves remain tantalizing mysteries. On a tour of Wind Cave, the park ranger at one point turns out all the artificial lights in a large limestone room.

"This is true darkness," he says. "You may think you've been in the dark before, but only in a cave like this can all light be extinguished." And it's true. On the surface there is always a glow from the house down the street, the moon, a star—but here the darkness seems complete enough to swallow you up.

Then the ranger turns on a special ultraviolet lamp, and its rays illumine the rock formations which glow with an eerie beauty.

Limestone "Donkey Ears"

There are many other caves in the Black Hills: Wildcat, Rushmore, Wonderland, Stagebarn, and others. Near Elk Canyon north of Rapid City is Bethlehem Cave, where Benedictine Fathers maintain the Shrine of the Nativity. Once known as Crystal Cave, the site was donated to the fathers by an elderly Black Hills man, Louis Storm.

The shrine was built in one of the cave rooms under the supervision of Father Gilbert Stack. Many-colored glass candleholders hang from the ceiling, representing the nations of the world and symbolizing prayers for peace.

An old mule barn near the cave has been converted into living quarters for the monks. The barn also houses a post office which is entitled to use the cancellation Bethlehem, S. Dak. At Christmastime thousands of cards are sent here to be postmarked in that way.

Men have altered the mountains in many ways in the last hundred years. They have dug for gold, carried on scientific research, explored caves, created parks and monuments. Nothing shows the hand of man at work more overwhelmingly than Gutzon Borglum's famous mountain sculpture: Mount Rushmore.

Chapter 8

The Shrine of Democracy

They look down on the surrounding gulches and valleys like specimens of some prehistoric race of giants: four men who shaped American history and served as American Presidents.

Washington is there, the man who, more than any other, guided the United States in its first independent steps. Jefferson is next, the author of the Declaration of Independence, philosopher and statesman, the President who bought the vast Lousiana Territory, including Dakota, in 1803. Lincoln broods over the nation his leadership preserved as a union of free and equal men. And Theodore Roosevelt, representative of the new challenges and accomplishments of the twentieth century, completes the picture.

Mount Rushmore National Memorial is a unique tribute to four great men. Each head is about 60 feet high, on a scale of a man 465 feet tall. The memorial is known as the Shrine of Democracy.

Mount Rushmore National Memorial

Shortly after the Black Hills gold rush, a New York lawyer named Charles E. Rushmore visited the hills to look after the mining interests of one of his clients. While touring in a horse and buggy, the attorney asked the name of a particular granite peak. "Mount Rushmore," joked a member of the party, and the name stuck. But no one at that time envisioned the use that would later be made of it.

The mountain had two advantages for a large sculpture: It was composed of smooth-grained granite, and it faced the sun during much of the day, providing natural lighting.

In 1924 South Dakota historian Doane Robinson proposed the idea of a large monument carved in Black Hills granite. Other South Dakotans responded to the suggestion, and an inquiry was sent to sculptor Gutzon Borglum, who was then working on a large Confederate memorial at Stone Mountain, Georgia.

Borglum, the son of a Danish immigrant, grew up in Idaho. He studied art in Paris and Spain, and he was already a well-known sculptor when Doane Robinson wrote to him. Borglum's head of Lincoln is displayed in the rotunda of the Capitol Building in Washington, D.C.

In September of 1924 Gutzon Borglum came to visit the Black Hills, accompanied by his small son, Lincoln. Originally, the idea was to honor some local hero with a statue carved somewhere in the Needles area. But touring the hills, Borglum began to think in grander terms. He envisioned a monument for the whole nation, and on a vast scale.

He chose Mount Rushmore and created a model showing the four faces he intended to carve there. In the beginning money was raised through private contributions, but as more funds were required the federal government assumed the financial responsibility for the memorial.

In August, 1927, President Calvin Coolidge dedicated the memorial, and work began. Borglum built a studio with a large plate-glass window facing Mount Rushmore. Here he worked on his models, continuously changing them as he studied the mountain and its granite surface.

The carving of Mount Rushmore took fourteen years. Light

78

charges of dynamite were used to blast out the rock, and the finishing touches were done by hand. Complex scaffolding was built of heavy timber. Workmen also were lowered over the side of the mountain from harnesses, or bosun's chairs, controlled by hand-operated winches.

Measurements from Borglum's models had to be transferred to the mountain on a one-to-twelve scale. The point of the nose was located first, then the other features placed around it.

Gutzon Borglum died seven months before the memorial was finished. His son, Lincoln Borglum, who had come with him to the Black Hills as a boy, continued the project until funds were expended in October of 1941.

Since then, millions of people have come to see South Dakota's Shrine of Democracy. A visitors' center has been built, and National Park Service rangers tell the history of the carving and the

Sculptor Korczak Ziolkowski with his model of Crazy Horse

Maintenance man at work, Mount Rushmore National Memorial

four Presidents depicted there. Each night during the summer months a special ceremony is held as the lights are turned on to illumine the monument.

Mount Rushmore is estimated to be between 500,000,000 and 1,000,-000,000 years old. Its granite is unusually strong and long-lasting. Borglum hoped that his carving would be "a messenger to posterity ten thousand, one hundred thousand, or . . . a million years hence." He saw it as a word from our time to the future: This we stood for; this we believed in.

In spite of its durability, Mount Rushmore requires regular maintenance. Each year a crew of men inspects the monument thoroughly. Cracks which exist in the face of the mountain are carefully patched with a mixture developed by Gutzon Borglum himself: equal parts of linseed oil, white lead, and powdered granite.

Maintenance crews are lowered over the face of the carving by hoists controlled from the top. They move from side to side by taking up or releasing guy lines attached to their safety belts and secured to steel pins on the mountain.

It is unlikely that any more faces will ever be added to Mount Rushmore. Borglum stated as the monument neared completion that there was no carvable granite left on the mountain.

Another mountain sculpture is under way in the Black Hills, honoring one of the original Americans: Crazy Horse, the Oglala Sioux chief and leader of the Indians who wiped out Custer's Seventh Cavalry at the Little Big Horn.

The idea of a statue of Crazy Horse was conceived by Chief Henry Standing Bear. Chief Standing Bear suggested the project to sculptor Korczak Ziolkowski, who had worked briefly on the Mount Rushmore carving.

Ziolkowski, a Polish orphan who grew up in Boston, was impressed by Standing Bear's letter which said: "My fellow chiefs and I would like the white people to know that the Redmen had great heroes too."

Thunderhead Mountain near Custer was chosen as the site of the monument. Plans call for the figure of the Sioux chief to be shown mounted on a horse. The carving will be on a gigantic scale—nearly 600 feet high by 700 feet long.

After service in World War II, Korczak Ziolkowski came to South Dakota and bought a dilapidated ranch at the foot of Thunderhead Mountain. He began blasting in 1948. Funds for the project come from tourists, who pay admission to see the sculptor's home and studio; from private donations; and some of the profits from a dairy herd of registered Holstein cows.

Mr. Ziolkowski also plans to establish an Indian museum, medical center and university at the base of Thunderhead Mountain.

Mount Rushmore, main terrace

The Crazy Horse project has been ridiculed by some. It will certainly take many years to bring the dream to reality. The sculptor has already blasted off eight times as much rock as was removed from Mount Rushmore during the carving of that monument.

But Thunderhead Mountain and South Dakota have already been changed by the bearded artist from Massachusetts. His work serves as a reminder of the dignity and worth of the culture of the Dakota Indians which existed here before the white man.

Chapter 9

The Old Ways

The great grandfather
has said
so they report
Dakotas
be citizens
he said
so they report
but
it will be impossible
the Dakota ways
them
I love
I said
therefore
I have helped to keep
the old ways.

Chief Sitting Bull

This Sioux Indians' song expresses the sadness caused by a clash between two cultures. The old ways were good; the new ways seem strange and sometimes not so good. It is impossible to go back to former times, but it is also very difficult to move into a future decided for you by others.

In order to understand the life and problems of modern-day South Dakota Indians, it is necessary to know something about the roots from which they come.

There have been many different Indian tribes in the United States, with different ways of life, dress, housing and so forth. But somehow when anyone wants to "dress like an Indian" today he dons the typical clothing of the Great Plains tribes. We think of Indians as living in tepees, riding horseback, with braided hair and beaded shirts—all part of the "old ways" of the ancestors of today's South Dakota Indians.

The names Sioux and Dakota are now used interchangeably for the tribes that dominated Dakota when the white men came. Sioux was originally a Chippewa word used to mean "snake" or "enemy." The name Dakota was what the tribes called themselves; it means "an alliance of friends." The Dakota Indians were bound together by ties of religion, family and deep affection. Theirs was a society in which every member of the tribes had a place. Everyone was valued and respected.

Their religion identified man with nature. Man was intended to live in harmony with nature. He had to take his place in the scheme of things and to express his respect for the tremendous forces of the natural world. Religion was not separate from the rest of an Indian's life but affected his every attitude and action.

The basis of Dakota Indian society was the family. This was not the sort of family we think of today: father, mother, children. The Indian "extended family" or *tiyospaye* also included grandparents, aunts and uncles. The male child called his father's brother "father" and his mother's sister "aunt." The female child called her mother's sister "mother."

Within this large family everyone knew exactly what was expected of him. Even the tone of voice in which to address a grandfather, sister, or mother-in-law was established. You might do a great deal of joking with some members of the family but keep an attitude of great respect with others.

All members of the family had their work to do; all shared the food and other goods. Only horses were regarded as personal property. Indians did not judge each other's worth by ownership of things, but only by the skill with which those things were used.

Men were the defenders and providers. They gave protection from enemies and wild animals, and their hunting brought the provisions the family needed. The women cared for the children, prepared food and clothing, nursed the old and the sick.

An older and highly respected man was looked up to as the head of the family. Dakota Indian chiefs were not all-powerful leaders, for all men were considered basically equal.

Children were particularly valued by the Dakotas. They were given much love and affection by all members of the family, and physical punishment was unknown. Discipline was established through the child's desire to be a respected part of the group.

Many people think of Indians as stony, unemotional people. Actually, they expressed their feelings more freely than most white people do today.

Four virtues made up the moral code of the Dakotas: bravery, endurance, generosity, and integrity. A person was expected to give up his own life, if necessary, for the good of his family group or tribe. Courage was shown not only in battle but in sickness, tragedy, and old age.

The ideal of generosity created a custom which seems strange to non-Indians: the "give-away." When some person was to be honored his relatives would hold a feast and give away nearly everything they had. Selfishness was considered a great evil, and no one would refuse to help the needy. Most things were shared freely, and each person simply took what he needed.

The Indian culture provided security, love, and acceptance for each individual. It served the people well while they were free to roam the Great Plains.

But the white man came. At first the Indians were not quite sure what to make of him. Some of the early missionaries such as Roman Catholic Father De Smet and Congregationalist Stephen Riggs seemed friendly and helpful. French fur trappers intermarried with the Indians and adopted their ways. But as more and more white people poured into Dakota Territory, the Indians sensed a serious threat.

The land over which they had hunted at will was being cut up into farms and towns. Soldiers came to protect the settlers, and they had the habit of punishing one group of Indians for the deeds of another. Treaties were made and broken. And, most serious of all, the buffalo were slaughtered.

The Indians never wasted land or animals. They killed only what they needed, and used every part of the buffalo. They were repelled by the extermination of these animals, many of which were left to

Plains encampment of the Assiniboine Indians, a century ago.

rot; by the pollution of streams and rivers; by the destruction of beaver dams and killing of birds.

When gold was discovered in the Black Hills, thousands of white men rushed to the scene, disregarding the recent treaty which made the hills part of Indian Territory. The Sioux resisted, and in the famous Battle of the Little Big Horn wiped out one of the government troop detachments that had been sent to force them back on reservations. But there were too many white men, and the Indians could not hold them back for long.

Ben Black Elk remembered the events that followed this way:

Wherever we went, the soldiers came to kill us, and it was all our own country. It was ours already when the Wasichus made the

treaty with Red Cloud, that said it would be ours as long as grass should grow and water flow. That was only eight winters before, and they were chasing us now because we remembered and they forgot.

So the proud Sioux were sent to live on reservations. Government handouts replaced the vanished buffalo. Food was often late in arriving; several times the Indians were at the point of starvation in winter when the government beef or flour finally came through.

An attempt was made to turn the Indians into farmers. But the land which had been allotted to them was poor, and the Sioux had no tradition of agriculture. Their men had been hunters and fighters. The idea of farming seemed degrading, and even those who did try found the results poor in the hot, dry climate.

Each Indian head of a family was allotted 160 acres of land on the reservation as part of this attempt to encourage farming. This method tended to break up the traditional extended family groups of the Indians into smaller units consisting of father, mother, and children.

Education was seen as the best way to help Indians adapt to white culture. It was felt that Indian children had to be taken out of their home environment in order to make the break from the Indian ways. So boarding schools were set up by the Bureau of Indian Affairs. This, too, tended to break up the strong family ties which had given purpose and security in the old days.

White men's diseases added to the Indians' problems. Smallpox, measles, whooping cough and "grippe" often struck them much more severely than their white neighbors because they had built up no resistance to those diseases.

In 1890 a new religion became popular among the Dakota Sioux. It foretold the coming of an Indian messiah, who would bring back the buffalo, drive out the white men, and destroy the diseases that were weakening the Indians.

The heart of the new religion was the Ghost Dance. Before this ceremony the dancers purified themselves in a sweat lodge filled with steam. Then they dressed in "ghost shirts" marked with religious symbols, which were thought to protect them from soldiers' bullets.

The Indians danced around a small tree with an American flag at the top. They chanted songs such as this one:

> The whole world is coming,
> A nation is coming, a nation is coming,
> The Eagle has brought the message to the tribe.
> The father says so, the father says so.
> Over the whole earth they are coming.
> The buffalo are coming, the buffalo are coming . . .

The messiah cult might have died out harmlessly, but some of the white settlers and agents were frightened by it. They called in the soldiers.

A band of Sioux led by Big Foot fled into the Badlands after Chief Sitting Bull had been killed by federal troops. The Seventh Cavalry intercepted them and marched them to a camp at Wounded Knee Creek. On December 28, 1890, as the soldiers were disarming the Indians, there was a scuffle, and shooting broke out.

What followed has been called the Battle of Wounded Knee, but it was more a slaughter than a battle. Nearly 200 Indians—men, women, and children—were killed. Soldiers followed those who fled and shot them as they ran.

Wounded Knee was the last major clash between federal troops and American Indians. It marked the end of the Ghost Dances, and the end of any real hope of returning to the past.

South Dakota Indians went back to the reservations and began trying to make the best of things. Some did well as ranchers and cattlemen. Some attained higher education, left the reservations and found a place in American society. But for most of the descendants of the Dakotas, home is still the Pine Ridge, Rosebud, Cheyenne River, Lower Brule, Crow Creek, Yankton, Sisseton, Flandreau, or Standing Rock Reservation.

These reservations make up a large and unique part of modern South Dakota. A blend of the old ways and the new, they are still changing as the original owners of Dakota try to find their place in the space age.

Chapter 10

The Reservations

PINE RIDGE INDIAN RESERVATION, the map says.

You see no encircled tepees, no feathered warriors, no tomahawks or spears. The land is like the rest of South Dakota's West-river ranchland—open, rolling and grass-covered. The occasional small house is set back from the highway. Most of the towns consist of a few houses and stores, perhaps a small church. You may pass a group of Indian children walking beside the road, but they are dressed like any other rural children.

Pine Ridge is the most heavily populated of South Dakota's Indian reservations. Of course, Indians are not required to live on any of these reservations, and many of them have moved to larger towns such as Rapid City. But the reservation land which was given to the Indians by the government is still home to many of the Dakotas.

The old Indian ways have not vanished completely. The Dakota

A war dance of the Plains Indians

language is still spoken in many homes. Family ties are strong and extend to the most distant relatives. The ideal of sharing and generosity is practiced. The names of the people reflect their heritage: Yellow Robe, Black Hawk, Hollow Horn Bear, White Buffalo, Chasing Horse.

But the way of life which the Indian culture served so well is gone. The reservations are only islands in the white man's world, and the new ways cannot be shut out.

The values of Indian life conflict in many ways with those of white society. To the Dakotas, the idea of accumulating material goods for personal use is selfish and revolting. A set of values based on things is foreign to their way of seeing life in terms of human relationships. White people seem to care less about each other than about wealth and power.

When solemn treaties were repeatedly broken by the land-hungry and the gold seekers, Indians decided that the whites are people who "break their own taboos." The moral teachings of the missionaries sounded worthy, but they did not seem to be carried out by the majority of the whites.

The Dakota culture was ancient and slow to change. This made it even harder for Indians to adapt themselves to the dynamic, constantly changing white civilization. In some ways the strides of science in the last few years have cut them off even more from the rest of America.

The people of the reservations have many problems to overcome. Most obvious of these is the low economic level at which they live. A recent survey showed that more than half the heads of families at Pine Ridge were unemployed. Only about 2 percent of the families had incomes of more than $5,000 a year.

Reservation land is not capable of supporting all the people who live there. And most Indians lack the skills to compete for jobs off the reservations.

The educational program of the Bureau of Indian Affairs helped some. One older Indian told of his experience in this way: "I was about seven or eight years old when they came to take me to government boarding school. I can see my mother standing there. I was hanging on to her skirts, and they had to pull me away. They had a hard time breaking my hold. I screamed—'Don't let them take me away!' I cried myself to sleep for weeks in that lonely boarding school.

"Actually, it turned out to be the best thing that happened to me. I got all the education that it was possible to get at that time. The teachers were wonderful people. They taught us the things that we needed to know and to do in the white culture. Had I not been literally dragged away from home, things would have been very different for me."

This man broke away from the Indian culture. He married a non-Indian, sent his children to school and college, and never taught them the Dakota language. He became "like a white man."

Others were not so willing to break with the past. Family affection was strong; the outside world was strange and sometimes hostile. The weakness of the boarding school system was that it worked against the influence of home and family which had always been so important to the Indians.

Schools have been established on the reservations so that the Indian children do not have to leave home to get an education. But this system, too, has problems. Children may do very well in the early years and then lose interest as they reach the upper grades, junior high and high school. The idea of competition for grades which spurs many whites to achievement in school does not appeal to Indian children. Parents are not often involved in the process of education and so may not encourage their children to keep up attendance and homework.

Poor health may also interfere with schoolwork. Indian diet was healthy in the old days, but modern Indians have often adopted the wrong elements of white men's food. An Indian child whose diet consists mainly of bread and soda pop is unlikely to be able to keep up with a challenging program of education. Hot lunches at school and the teaching of proper nutrition to parents may help to change this situation. But the present low standard of living will have to be raised, too, before all Indian young people feel the glow of being really healthy.

Sioux Indian woman holding baby in cradleboard

As they grow older, Indian children become more aware of the world around them. Seeing something of life off the reservation, they begin to think of themselves as "different." Knowing they may be discriminated against or looked down on, they fear trying to make a place in white society. Stranded between two cultures, they are not completely at home in either. The old values have lost meaning. But new values have not replaced them, and so they may feel empty, without direction.

Another problem is that if an Indian does become educated and begin to earn a good living, he may soon be supporting a large number of relatives. This is expected under the old tradition of sharing. So in order to succeed on white terms, an Indian will probably have to reject his own culture, and lose the respect of his family.

Although Indians are United States citizens, they govern themselves on the reservations through specially elected tribal councils. Indian police patrol the reservations, and Indian courts judge misdemeanors committed there.

A distinction may be made between "full-bloods" and "mixed-bloods." Some small communities on the Pine Ridge Reservation such as Calico Hall, Wolf Creek, Wounded Knee, and Porcupine are made up mostly of full-blooded Sioux Indians. Old customs tend to be stronger in these communities, and the use of the Dakota language more common.

In larger towns near the reservations such as White River, Kadoka, Mission, Martin, and Winner, population includes many white people. Indians in these communities are more exposed to outside influences, less apt to keep the old ways.

In spite of the many difficulties they face, Sioux Indians have made a contribution to South Dakota and to the whole United States.

Benjamin Reifel, First District Congressman from South Dakota, is the first American Indian ever elected to the Congress of the United States. One of this country's most noted Indian artists is Oscar Howe, whose paintings of Dakota ceremonies and history have been widely exhibited. Billy Mills won a gold medal for the United States in the 10,000-meter run at the Olympics in Japan in 1964. Ella Deloria is a nationally known anthropologist.

Many other Indians have become educated and returned to the reservations to serve as teachers, ministers, social workers, or employees of the Bureau of Indian Affairs.

Today many South Dakotans, Indian and white, are beginning to feel that the Dakota culture should be preserved rather than wiped out. Efforts are being made to teach Indian youngsters pride in their history and heritage. And it seems likely that this heritage has some positive values to offer the whole of America.

Indian family loyalty, affection for children, generosity and unselfishness have already been discussed. Their traditional respect for older people and their sense of harmony with nature are worthwhile qualities often lacking in the twentieth century.

The old customs draw Indian people together in a close fellowship. For instance, when someone has a new house, there is often a dedication ceremony. Friends and relatives gather, and without any announcements or planned program everyone knows what to do. There are prayers; a meal is shared. When the meal is over no one has to tap a water glass or call for attention. Thank-offering gifts are given, and again the people seem to know when the ceremony is over without being told.

Mrs. David Workman of White River is acquainted with many of the Rosebud Reservation Indians. "They have a time for talk and a time for silence," she observes. "Indians seem to be more sensitive

Rosebud Sioux Reservation today

to each other and the slightest gesture or shrug, while white people take their cue from words."

Indian children often have special artistic talents. This may be partly due to the fact that they are very much at home in the out-of-doors and have been trained to observe and appreciate nature. Many Indian youngsters also excel in athletics.

The question facing modern South Dakota is how these positive qualities can be preserved while at the same time the Dakotas take a more active part in the future of the state. There cannot be one single answer. Education, job training, economic opportunities, better housing and improved health—all will play a part.

One hopeful sign is the development of industries on the reservations. At Pine Ridge, the Dakota Moccasin Factory employs many local Indians. The Pine Ridge Reservation Development Company is building a large industrial park. A fishhook factory employs many Pine Ridge Indians, and others will find jobs at a new center for the sale of arts and crafts.

The Rosebud Manufacturing Company on the Rosebud Reservation produces laminated plastic, and a frozen food company may locate there soon. Similar projects on the other reservations make it likely that unemployment will go down, and the standard of living will rise in the future.

Reservation housing has been greatly improved by the construction of government-financed homes. These new homes, known as "transitional housing," are small but attractive and sturdy. Not long ago many Indians still lived in tents and abandoned cars, but the new housing program is helping to give each family adequate shelter.

For those who wish to move away from the reservations, the Bureau of Indian Affairs has a program of financial aid for moving, finding housing and employment or vocational training. The state of South Dakota also offers seventy-five college scholarships to South Dakotans with one-quarter or more Indian blood.

The Sioux Indians are part of the people of South Dakota. But the state includes people of many different cultural backgrounds. Nearly everyone is a part of some minority group, and each of these has played its part in the making of South Dakota.

99

Chapter 11

The People

Except for the Indians, few of South Dakota's minority groups have been in the state for more than a hundred years. South Dakota has no long history of colonization and waves of migration blending to form a new people. Because of this, distinct national groups could still be seen in many parts of the state until quite recently.

The largest national group in South Dakota is the Scandinavian. People of Norwegian, Swedish and Danish background came to Dakota Territory when it was first opened for settlement. Their homesteads in eastern South Dakota laid the original foundations of the organized state.

In 1927 O. E. Rolvaag published a book called *Giants in the Earth,* based on his experiences as a boy in early-day South Dakota. Originally written in Norwegian, it has been translated into English and is one of the most famous novels about pioneer life.

"Jedediah Smith in the Badlands," painted by Harvey Dunn

The characters in *Giants in the Earth* are strong, quiet people who have to deal with the terrible loneliness of the prairies. Some of them finally are broken by the fear and strangeness of the new land. Some perish in the blizzards, and some return to more settled places. But there are those who stay.

South Dakota's telephone books are full of Scandinavian names. Foods like lefse and lutefisk are popular throughout the state. Many small East-river towns are made up almost entirely of Norwegian Americans or Swedish Americans.

Most of the Scandinavians came to South Dakota as homesteaders, and many of them are still farmers. This is also true of the next largest group of South Dakotans—the Germans.

Like the Swedes, Danes and Norwegians, the Germans came to Dakota Territory as homesteaders when it was first opened for settlement. Some of them also belonged to religious groups which had been persecuted in Europe. The Hutterite Brethren established agricultural colonies in the James River valley, and twenty-four of their colonies exist in modern South Dakota.

The Hutterites are followers of Jacob Hutter, a Moravian preacher who was burned at the stake for his teachings in 1536. His followers fled first to Russia, and then from Russia to the United States. Some of their basic beliefs are adult baptism, separation of church and state, pacifism, and the sharing of material wealth.

Hutterites established their first American colony at Bon Homme, South Dakota, in 1874. This colony a few miles west of Yankton is still active.

Unlike some other communal farmers in the United States, the Hutterites use modern tools and methods. Each of the colonies is self-sufficient. Communal buildings cluster in the middle of the land-holdings: a machine shop, barns, granaries, apartments, a dining hall. The people live in simply furnished rooms and eat all their meals together. Men are divided into work crews and are used where they are needed. The Hutterites practice soil conservation and are efficient farmers.

Married men have full beards and wear clothes of black denim. The women wear long-sleeved blouses, full skirts and head scarves.

The colonies maintain their own schools for the education of children.

Because they are pacifists, the Hutterites serve their military obligation as conscientious objectors.

All the colonies raise cattle, hogs, chickens, and other poultry. The basic crops, as in the rest of eastern South Dakota, are corn, sorghum, wheat and oats. Many of the colonies also keep bees.

Hutterite colonies now extend the length of the James River. The average colony has about 14 families and 100 people. When a colony reaches about 150, it divides and starts a new colony.

The Hutterites are only a small portion of the German people who came to South Dakota, but their customs have been preserved through isolation. Many other people of German ancestry became farmers, businessmen, lawyers, teachers and carpenters, throughout the state of South Dakota.

Slavic people also took part in the move to Dakota Territory when the land was opened for homesteading. Bohemians have been an especially strong group in the southeastern part of the state.

Until a few years ago the majority of the residents of Tabor, South Dakota, spoke Bohemian at home. The language is still heard frequently on the streets of Tabor. A musical and fun-loving people, the Bohemians are famous for their dancing and playing the concertina.

Each summer Tabor hosts a celebration called Czech Days. Local people dress in Bohemian costumes and perform dances such as the difficult Beseda.

A special contribution of the Slavs to South Dakota was their experimentation with fruit trees and orchards.

Sizable numbers of Dutch, English, Irish, Scottish and French people also settled in South Dakota through the years. And today most of the other cultures of America are also represented: Jews, Italians, Japanese, Negroes, Syrians, Swiss, Greeks.

Few South Dakotans today are descended from only one national group. Like Americans in other parts of the country, they have intermarried and grown away from the older customs and languages.

The people of South Dakota are rural in experience and outlook.

103

Czechoslovakian national dance

There is no city in the state of more than 100,000 people. A typical South Dakotan has a farm or small-town background.

A South Dakota childhood might include long bike rides on country roads, showing 4-H projects at county fairs, baseball and basketball, ice skating, picnics, hayrides, hunting and fishing. Farm children are expected to do their share of chores, learn to take care of animals and harvest crops.

Movies, radio and television, records and books are important to South Dakota youngsters as they are in the rest of the country.

The openness of the land itself gives South Dakotans a rural outlook. They grow up with wide skies and long, empty roads. Many of them later move to the great cities of America, but they carry with them the memory of those long horizons.

Children at Czech festival

Hubert Humphrey, former Vice President of the United States, is a native South Dakotan. The Humphrey Drug Store in Huron is still operated by members of his family.

Joe Foss, World War II hero and former governor of South Dakota, was the first commissioner of the American Football League.

The weekly newspaper at Aberdeen was once edited and published by L. Frank Baum, creator of the *Wizard of Oz* books.

Hamlin Garland was a homesteader in Brown County and clerked in his father's store at Ordway. His realistic stories of the frustrations and struggles of pioneer life—*A Son of the Middle Border, A Daughter of the Middle Border* and others—are American classics.

Harvey Dunn grew up in Kingsbury County, the son of home-

"Search for the Land of Milk and Honey," painted by Harvey Dunn

steaders. He left South Dakota and became a nationally famous artist and illustrator. His paintings of the battlefields of World War I are especially well known.

But Dunn never forgot South Dakota. And his art captured the feel of the country in an unforgettable way. Paintings like "Dakota Woman," "The Sunlit Hills," "The Prairie Is My Garden," and "School Day's End" speak of the people of South Dakota, what they have made of the land and what the land has made of them.

Laura Ingalls Wilder also lived in Kingsbury County, South Dakota. Her books capture in words what Dunn put into his paintings. Anyone who has read *The Long Winter* knows something of South Dakotans.

Though they are a rural people, they are not uneducated "hicks." In fact, the state has one of the highest literacy rates in the United States.

For many years the one-room schoolhouse was a common sight. Now most of these have been closed, school districts reorganized, and larger central schools built. There are seven state-supported and six private colleges in South Dakota. These colleges and universities are large enough to offer a variety of courses but small enough to allow for individual attention.

South Dakota people read the same books and magazines, watch the same television programs and hear the same newscasts as the rest of the country. If the state was once isolated, it cannot be now. Its citizens drive to Denver, Minneapolis or Chicago; fly to the West Coast; take a boat to Europe or Asia.

What are South Dakotans like? They are like other Americans. They work hard, worry about war and taxes, raise families. History has made them tough and independent, perhaps a little slow to change. Their experiences, their racial and national backgrounds make a pattern which is, more than the land or the towns or the businesses, South Dakota.

Chapter 12

Land of Infinite Variety

South Dakota is a mountainous state, a prairie state. It is land-locked and dry; it has hundreds of miles of shoreline. It belongs to the past and the future, to history and to modern times.

One of the most popular nicknames for South Dakota is The Land of Infinite Variety. Perhaps "infinite" is too strong a word, but surely South Dakota is a land of variety.

Each of the state's three major parts—Prairie Plains, Great Plains and Black Hills—is quite different from the others. Each section of South Dakota has its major interests. East of the Missouri, life centers on farming and manufacturing. In the West-river country, ranching is most important. And the Black Hills bases its economy on tourism and mining.

The job of the state government is to help all these different parts of South Dakota to work together. When the legislature meets in

Big Bend Dam, Fort Thompson, South Dakota

Harvesting hay at Sky Ranch

Pierre every spring, senators and representatives from all over the state try to work out their problems and find ways to improve the lives of all the people.

How much of the money for schools should come from state aid? What sort of taxes should be used to raise money? Should South

Dakota's small towns be allowed to die as population shifts to cities and roads bypass them? How can the civil rights of Indians and other groups be protected? Should capital punishment be abolished?

These are a few of the problems the South Dakota legislature must consider, with the advice of the governor and other officials.

The land of infinite variety is also a land of great possibilities. No one can be sure what the future will be, but there is room for much development in the years ahead.

South Dakota does not have to deal with some of the enormous problems of more urban states. Big-city rioting and crime, air pollution, overcrowding, and traffic snarls are not major considerations in a state like South Dakota. The energies of government and individuals may be spent in other areas.

More urgent problems in South Dakota are better prices for farm and ranch products; the future of the family farm and small town; increased educational opportunities; poverty on Indian reservations and in other parts of the state; attracting industries to provide more jobs.

In spite of these problems, South Dakota has some important plus marks. The future seems to be bright in several fields.

Oil and minerals offer possibilities for new sources of income for South Dakota. In addition to the gold of the Black Hills, the state has rich deposits of feldspar, mica and bentonite.

In northwestern South Dakota there is lignite or coal. The United States Geological Survey has estimated that Harding and Perkins counties contain 1,000,000,000 tons of lignite.

Oil has also been found in Harding County, and along the western border of South Dakota uranium is being mined. Increased use of these minerals, or the discovery of more deposits, may affect South Dakota's future in the years to come.

The raising of livestock has always been of major importance in South Dakota. But the nation's beef requirements will be increasing rapidly in the next twenty years or so, due to the expanding population and a trend to more meat in the diet. This will mean more demand for South Dakota beef. It will mean more business for ranchers, operators of feedlots, and meat-packers.

111

South Dakota has never been a center for heavy industry. Transportation expenses have prevented outside manufacturers from setting up plants in the state. But efforts are being made to attract more industry, and a recent study indicated that conditions are favorable for the development of increased manufacturing.

One reason is the pressure of overcrowding in America's larger cities. If the population continues to explode as predicted, Americans will need space to live and work. Someday South Dakota's richest resource may be its miles of open land.

Thoughts about the future must bring us back to the place where this story began—the river.

The control and development of the Missouri River provide a key to things to come in South Dakota. Since the first white men came here one major factor has limited people and their projects. This was the lack of rain. The Great American Desert was not exactly a desert, but it was too dry to produce crops like states to the east.

Now, suddenly, the four Missouri River dams have provided a chain of huge, inland lakes or reservoirs. Plans are being made for the irrigation of nearly 200,000 acres of land with water from the reservoirs. And this may be only the beginning.

Water is needed by farmers. Water may help attract new industries which would not have considered locating in South Dakota before. Water can produce more grass for cattle and sheep, and support more wildlife. Water can be used for low-cost electric power. Water provides a habitat for fish.

Before the dams were built, fishing in South Dakota was mostly limited to a few trout streams and small lakes. Now, the transformed Missouri abounds with fish. White bass, walleye, sauger, and northern pike are there for sport fishing. Many other species fill the new lakes: bigmouth buffalo, carp, channel catfish, shovelnose sturgeon, goldeye, crappie, shortnose gar, paddlefish, freshwater drum.

Commercial fishing is an infant industry in South Dakota. Studies made by the Bureau of Commercial Fisheries, Fish and Wildlife Service of the Department of the Interior, show great potential. Oahe Reservoir, alone, could easily produce some 12,000,000 pounds of commercial fish each year.

South Dakota's commercial fishing season runs from April to December. The fish, mostly buffalo, carp, carpsucker, goldeye and catfish, are caught in nets. They are then taken to local plants where they are sorted, washed, cleaned, put in a preservative and packed in ice. They are then shipped by truck to markets in Iowa, Illinois and New York.

The cost of getting the fish to market, the need for finding more markets and for product development limit the growth of commercial fishing. But new uses are being found for so-called "rough" fish like the buffalo fish. Pet food, fish meal and fish protein concentrate are

Days of '76 festival, Deadwood, South Dakota

a few examples. Some underdeveloped nations use fish concentrate or fish flour as their chief source of protein. This may point to an opportunity for the South Dakota reservoirs to help solve problems of hunger and malnutrition throughout the world.

The river, with its history and its potential, winds through the infinite variety that is South Dakota. It goes not only from North Dakota to Nebraska but from old to new, and the state through which it goes is moving too.

Still, some things remain. The wide horizons are there which greeted Lewis and Clark in 1804. The sun shines, most days, out of the boundless blue sky which was here when the Black Hills erupted out of the crust of the earth.

An old Dakota Indian blessing might be South Dakota's greeting to visitors, and to its own people:

> May the sun rise well
> May the earth appear
> Brightly shone upon.

SOUTH DAKOTA PROFILE

Sunshine State
Coyote State
Blizzard State

GENERAL

Statehood November 2, 1889; fortieth state to join the Union

Area 77,047 square miles; sixteenth-ranking state

Population 680,514 (1960 census); fortieth-ranking state

Capital Pierre

Motto "Under God the People Rule"

Song "Hail, South Dakota"

Flower Pasqueflower

Tree Black Hills spruce

Bird Ring-necked pheasant

Animal Coyote

PHYSICAL CHARACTERISTICS

Boundaries

North North Dakota

East Minnesota and Iowa

West Wyoming and Montana

South Nebraska

Greatest width 204 miles

Greatest length 380 miles

Highest point 7,242 feet at Harney Peak

Lowest point 966 feet at Big Stone Lake

Climate

Sunny, dry; average year has 89 cloudy days; average temperature for January: 16°, for July: 72°; average precipitation 19.1 inches per year; highest recorded temperature: 120°; lowest recorded temperature:—58°

Principal cities

Sioux Falls: 65,466
  Largest city; center of retail and wholesale trade and transportation, meat-packing, journalism, education

Rapid City: 42,399
  Manufactures cement, flour, leather goods, concrete pipe; location of South Dakota School of Mines and Technology

Aberdeen: 23,073
  Important rail and wholesale merchandising center

Huron: 14,180
  Trading and tourism center; location of Huron College

Brookings: 10,558
  Creameries chief industry; location of South Dakota College of Agriculture and Mining

Pierre: 10,088
  State capital; shipping point for grain and livestock; bottling works and food processing plants; Oahe Dam located near here

Principal lakes and reservoirs

Angostura Reservoir	Big Stone Lake	Shadehill Reservoir
Belle Fourche Reservoir	Fort Randall Reservoir	Traverse Lake

Principal rivers

Big Sioux	Grand	Missouri	Vermillion
Cheyenne	James	Moreau	White

LEADING PRODUCTS

Industry

Processing of farm products: meat-packing, butter making, bakery products, flour and other milled grains; wood products

Agriculture

Small grains, corn, potatoes, flax; wheat; oats; spring wheat in the north, winter wheat in the south; alfalfa; beef cattle; sheep

Tourism

Now a leading industry, partly because of introduction of ring-necked pheasant

GOVERNMENT

U.S. Congress
Senators: 2
Representatives: 2

State Legislature
Senators: 35
Representatives: 75

Counties: 67
Electoral votes: 4

Universities and Colleges

Augustana College
Dakota Wesleyan University
Huron College
Sioux Falls College
South Dakota State College of
  Agriculture and Mining

South Dakota State School of
  Mines and Technology
State Teachers College located at Aberdeen
  Madison, Spearfish, Springfield
University of South Dakota
Yankton College

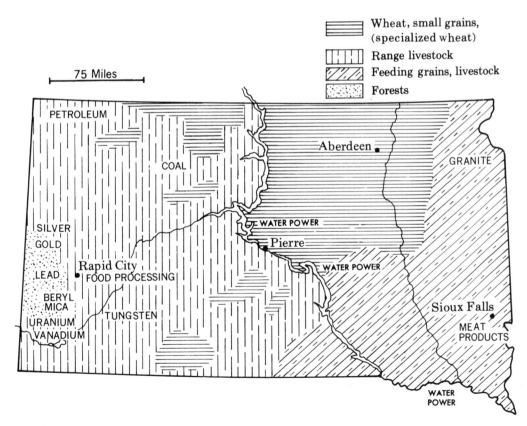

SOUTH DAKOTA – Resources

HISTORY

1200	Mound Builders known in South Dakota prior to this date.
1600	Arikaras, an agricultural Indian people, inhabited state.
1750–1790	Sioux drove Arikaras up the Missouri and into virtual extinction.
1742–1743	Vérendrye brothers came overland from Manitoba through Black Hills to Pierre.
1794	Jean-Baptiste Truteau had first building erected by white men in state; first building erected by explorers on banks of Missouri.
1803	Louisiana Purchase.
1804–1806	Lewis and Clark came up Missouri River, found few remaining Arikaras.
1817	Fort Teton built opposite modern site of Pierre; first white settlement in South Dakota.
1831	First steamboat, *Yellowstone,* reached site of Pierre.
1832	Fort Pierre built by American Fur Company.
1856	First attempt at permanent settlement, at falls of Sioux River.
1859	First permanent settlement, at Yankton.
1861	Dakota Territory created by Congress.
1873	Railway stage lines reach Yankton.
1874	Gold discovered in Black Hills by members of Custer's party on French Creek.
1876	Custer loses his life in Battle of the Little Big Horn, June 25.
1881–1886	Land boom.
1889	South Dakota granted statehood.
1890	Battle of Wounded Knee.
1896	Populist movement; William Jennings Bryan wins landslide in state for free silver campaign.
1917	State-operated rural credit system established.
1929	Depression.
1941–1945	World War II; nearly 60,000 South Dakota men and women in active service.
1940–1948	Period of prosperity; soil conservation programs, change in climate (heavy rains).
1944	Congress passes Flood Control Act and authorizes network of projects in upper Missouri Valley.
1949	Oahe reservoir and irrigation project started.
1952–1963	Four Missouri dams completed.

STATE GOVERNORS

TERRITORIAL

William Jayne	1861–1863
Newton Edmunds	1863–1866
Andrew J. Faulk	1866–1869
John L. Pennington	1874–1878
William A. Howard	1878–1880
Nehemiah G. Ordway	1880–1884
Gilbert A. Pierce	1884–1887
Louis A. Church	1887–1889
Arthur C. Mellette	1889

STATE

Arthur C. Mellette	1889–1893
Charles H. Sheldon	1893–1897
Andrew E. Lee	1897–1901
Charles M. Herreid	1901–1905
Samuel H. Elrod	1905–1907
Coe I. Crawford	1907–1909
Robert S. Vessey	1909–1913
Frank M. Byrne	1913–1917
Peter Norbeck	1917–1921
William H. McMaster	1921–1925
Carl Gunderson	1925–1927
William J. Bulow	1927–1931
Warren E. Green	1931–1933
Thomas Berry	1933–1937
Leslie Jensen	1937–1939
Harlan Bushfield	1939–1943
Merrell Q. Sharpe	1943–1947
George T. Mickelson	1947–1951
Sigurd Anderson	1951–1955
Joe J. Foss	1955–1959
Ralph Herseth	1959–1961
Archie Gubbrud	1961–1965
Nils Boe	1965–1969
Frank Farrar	1969–

PEOPLE AND SOUTH DAKOTA

This list does not necessarily include people identified in the book. You can find them in the index.

L. Frank Baum (1856–1917), author of *The Wizard of Oz* and many other children's books. Owned a variety store in Aberdeen, edited the weekly newspaper there.

W. H. Beadle (1837–1915), educator; influenced the new states of South Dakota, North Dakota, Montana, Washington, Wyoming and Idaho to set aside land for public schools.

Gutzon Borglum (1871–1941), sculptor of the Mount Rushmore monument.

Mary Jane Burke, "Calamity Jane" (1852–1901), famous frontier character in South Dakota gold-mining days in the 1870's.

James Butler "Wild Bill" Hickok (1837–1876), famous soldier, scout, law enforcement officer.

Crazy Horse (1847–1877), Oglala chief; resisted white settlers; fought with Sitting Bull against Custer at Big Horn.

Niels E. Hansen (1866–1950), educator, horticulturist; traveled throughout the world finding specimens of plants that might thrive in the United States; developed many strains of fruits and grains now grown here.

William Hobard Hare (1838–1909), Episcopal bishop, missionary to the Sioux Indians; founded many schools for the Indian people of South Dakota.

Henry Langford Loucks (1846–1928), agrarian political leader.

George S. McGovern (1922–   ), United States Senator since 1962; head of the Food for Peace program under President John Kennedy.

Arthur Calvin Mellette (1842–1896), last territorial and first state governor.

Peter Norbeck (1870–1936), politician and conservationist; influenced the building and development of Custer State Park.

Richard Franklin Pettigrew (1848–1926), Dakota territorial delegate and first U.S. Senator from the state.

Red Cloud (1822–1909), Oglala Sioux chief; went to Washington, D.C., to confer with President Rutherford B. Hayes, led his people through the transition to life on reservations.

Sitting Bull (1834–1890), Sioux Indian leader who opposed Custer; arrested and killed during Ghost Dance craze.

Joseph Ward (1838–1889), clergyman and educator.

PRONUNCIATION GUIDE

Belle Fourche	bell *forsh*
Cheyenne	shy *an*
Chinook	shi *nook*
Couteau des Prairies	koo *toe* day *prer* eez
Huron	*hyur* on
Moreau	more *oh*
Paha Sapa	*pa* ha *sa* pa
Pierre	peer
Shenandoah	shen an *doh* a
Sihasapa	*see* ha *sa* pa
Sioux	soo
Sisseton	*si* suh ton
Teton	*tee* ton
Verendrye	*ve* run dree
Vermillion	ver *mil* yun
Wahpekute	wa pay *koo* tay
Wahpeton	wa *pay* ton
Yankton	*yank* ton
Yanktonais	*yank* ton *ay*

Index

ACKNOWLEDGMENTS

My thanks to the many individuals who helped me to obtain and verify information about South Dakota: Mrs. Dorothy Workman; Mrs. Mildred Fielder; Mr. and Mrs. Herb Conn; Mrs. Bjorn Bjornson of Northern States Power Company; Mrs. Harold Coe; Mr. Harold Shunk, former superintendent of the Rosebud Indian Reservation; Mr. Ted Husted of Wall Drug; Mrs. Ruth Ziolkowski; Dr. Morton Green of South Dakota School of Mines and Technology; Mr. Don Gillespie, Mr. Warren Hotchkiss, Mr. Wallace Elms, and Mr. Byron Hazeltine of the National Park Service; Mr. Joseph Higham, Jr., of the Fish and Wildlife Service; Mr. William L. Evans of the Forest Service; and the Department of Travel and Publicity, South Dakota Department of Highways.

Although she is a relative newcomer to the state, Nancy Veglahn writes of South Dakota with the enthusiasm of a tourist, coupled with the understanding and affection of a lifelong resident.

Mrs. Veglahn grew up in Sioux City, Iowa, and graduated from Morningside College there in 1959. She and her husband then moved to New Haven, Connecticut, where he attended the Yale University Divinity School. From there they went to South Dakota, and they now live with their two children in Brookings, in the eastern part of the state, where Mr. Veglahn serves as minister to the Methodist Church.

Nancy Veglahn has previously published three outstanding books for young readers: *The Tiger's Tail* (1964), *The Spider of Brooklyn Heights* (1967), and *Peter Cartwright* (1968).

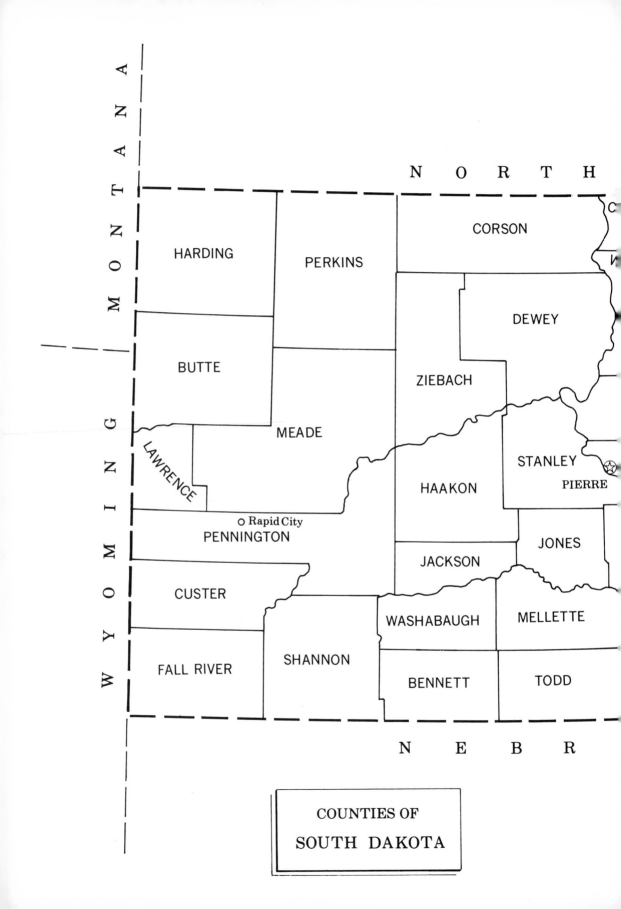

COUNTIES OF

SOUTH DAKOTA

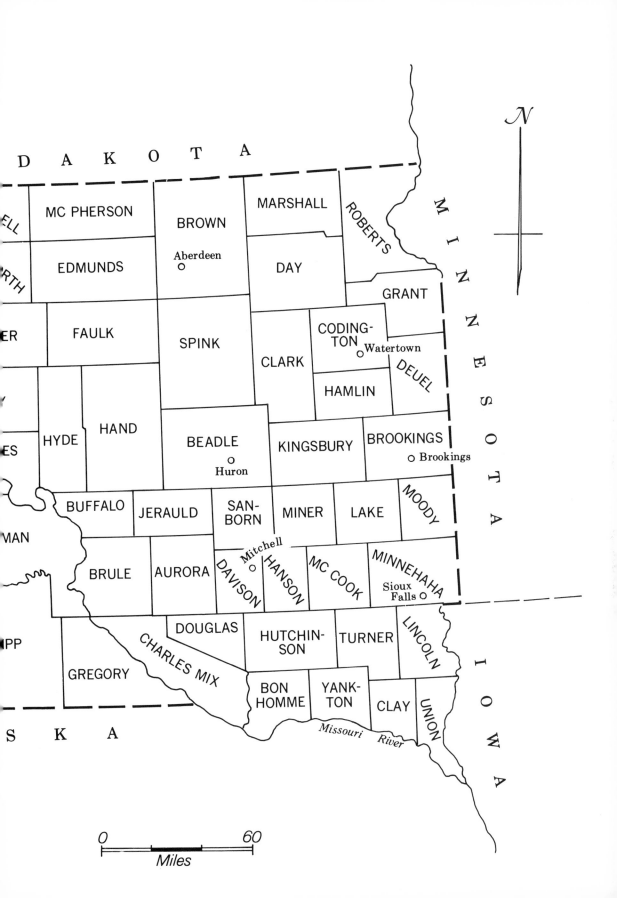

STATES OF THE NATION

These books provide young people with a contemporary survey of the economic life, character and resources of each of the states of the Union. They include salient events in the state's history, as well as the important facts about its geography, mineral wealth, peoples, parks, and recreational facilities. Each contains an extensive reference section which features a chronology of important moments in state history, a pronunciation guide to place-names, and a comprehensive index. And each is written in a narrative style which children will enjoy.

ALASKA
by Elsa Pedersen

ARIZONA
by Betty Baker

FLORIDA
by Mary Ellen Smith

INDIANA
by Jeannette C. Nolan

MASSACHUSETTS
by Margaret Coit

MICHIGAN
by Russel B. Nye

MONTANA
by Dorothy Johnson

NEW HAMPSHIRE
by Elizabeth Yates

NEW JERSEY
by Keith Robertson

NEW MEXICO
by Jack Schaefer

NEVADA
by Robert Laxalt

NORTH CAROLINA
by Thelma and Corydon Bell

OHIO
by Marion Renick

OREGON
by Iris Noble

RHODE ISLAND
by Scott Corbett

SOUTH CAROLINA
by Sally Edwards

SOUTH DAKOTA
by Nancy Veglahn

TENNESSEE
by William O. and
Allerton W. Steele

VIRGINIA
by Michael Frome

WASHINGTON
by Angelo M. Pellegrini

WEST VIRGINIA
by Felix Sutton

WISCONSIN
by August Derleth